BEADS, BUTTONS, AND BIJOUX

Nathalie Delhaye

photography by Akiko Ida

BEADS, BUTTONS, AND BIJOUX

58 Original Designs for Making Rings,
Necklaces, and Bracelets

POTTER
CRAFT
New York

SUPPLIES AND EQUIPMENT

BEADS

Beads come in a breathtaking array of materials, sizes, colors, and finishes. Before making your choice, read these notes and let your inspiration guide you. To help decide which materials and colors to use, scatter a selection of beads on a sheet of white paper and see what works well together.

BEAD SIZES

Due to their small size, beads are always measured in millimeters. If you cannot easily obtain the exact size of beads given in these projects, it is perfectly acceptable to use larger or smaller beads, adjusting the design as necessary.

Seed beads are measured in aughts, which represent the number of beads that can be lined up in a standard unit: an 8/o measurement means that 8 beads will fit in the space, while 11/o indicates that eleven beads will fit in the same amount of space. So the smaller the number, the bigger the bead, as it takes fewer beads to fill the standard space. The most common size available is 11/o, which generally has about 20 beads to the inch, while 8/o has 13 beads to the inch, and the tiny 15/o size has 25 beads to the inch. Sizes can vary according to manufacturer, country of origin, and finishes.

BUGLE BEADS (1)

Bugle beads are small, tubular-shaped glass beads which vary in length from 3 mm to 30 mm. Like seed beads, they are available in a wide variety of colors and finishes.

PLASTIC BEADS (2)

Plastic beads come in many shapes and colors, including deep shades. They are also lightweight.

SEED BEADS (3)

These are tiny, round glass beads from 1.5–4 mm in diameter. They can be transparent, opaque, matte, pearl, frosted, metallic, luster, silver- or color-lined, and come in hundreds of colors. Seed beads are often irregular, so you will need to choose them carefully, especially when making a row of beads that should match, as in a ring.

GLASS BEADS (4)

These heavy beads come in various shapes and sizes: faceted (such as Czech beads), rondelles, or teardrops. Lampwork glass beads (see photograph, page 81) are handmade by heating a rod of glass with a blowtorch and spinning the hot glass thread around a metal rod. Other layers of colored glass can be added to the surface to create many different designs.

CRYSTALS (5)

Crystals create a striking effect. Swarovski crystals are the best-known crystal, and are very popular for making rings. In this book you'll find other ways of using these gorgeous beads, whether they are faceted, round, cubes, bicones, or drops.

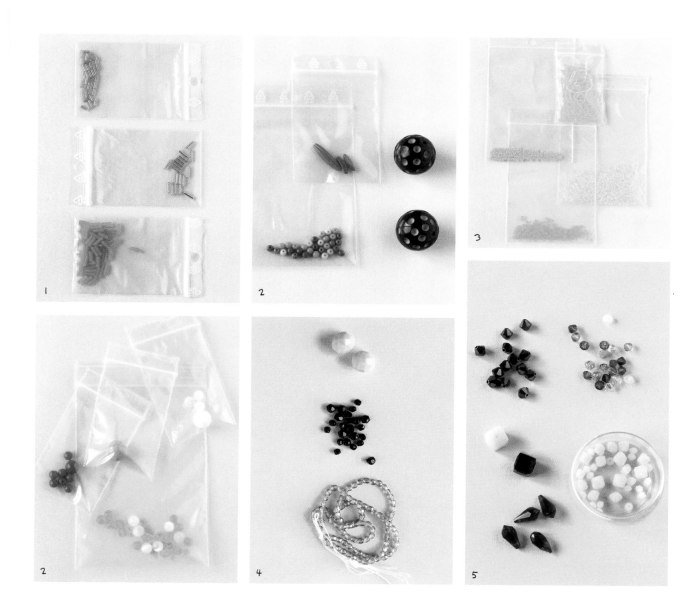

TOOLS

Pliers, glue, needles ... All the tools you need for these projects can be easily found in department stores and craft suppliers.

FLAT-NOSE PLIERS (1)

These are electrician's pliers. Select the smallest size possible. These pliers are indispensable, enabling you to grasp wire while stringing, to open and close rings, and to affix crimp beads.

CUTTERS (2)

Wire cutters will cut all stringing materials no matter what the thickness: soft-flex wire, jewelry wire, or eye and head pins.

ROUND-NOSE PLIERS (3)

Round-nose pliers are used for making a loop on an eye or head pin.

NEEDLES

An embroidery needle and a sewing needle will help you finish many wire-threading and jewelry projects.

GLUES

Most of the projects in this book use quick-drying glue. It can be used to strengthen an assembly, for example around crimp-covers. Use a tiny dot of quick-drying glue on the knot of a nylon thread to round off a row of beads for a ring.

1

2

3

STRINGING MATERIALS

There are many kinds of threads, cords, and wires in varying thicknesses and colors.
Your choice will depend on the desired effect and the type of ornament you want to create.

NYLON THREAD (1)

This comes in different colors and thicknesses. In these projects we mainly use size 0 (0.25 mm) thread. It is tough but unobtrusive, and has many advantages, as it is flexible and slightly stretchy. Nylon thread is very practical for making rings to fit the exact size of a finger. When using nylon thread, gently stretch it first—this pulls the coils out of the thread and helps to keep it from knotting and twisting.

METALLIC WIRE (2)

Of the many colors available, only gold, silver, or black jewelry wire is used in this book. Wire is perfect for making a rigid ornament. While easy to work with, jewelry wire is fragile and can easily become twisted (use flat-nose pliers to straighten) —it may even break if folded several times in the same place. In the United States, wire is measured in gauge (also spelled gage), while in Europe, it is measured in millimeters.

SOFT-FLEX WIRE (3)

This is stainless-steel-braided wire coated with nylon. It is available in silver, gold, and other colors. Soft-flex wire is strong, and therefore perfect for stringing heavy beads or decorations. To anchor a bead on this wire, use a crimp bead (see "Findings," page 10), and close it with flat-nose pliers.

POLYESTER THREAD

This sewing thread comes in many colors and can be used both for sewing and stringing.

PLASTIC LACING (4)

Hollow plastic lacing (Scoubidou or Scoubi) is available from craft suppliers and comes in a multitude of colors, making it useful for a wide range of projects limited only by your imagination. It is good for covering thread. If you find it hard to obtain, try the numerous craft supplier sites on the Web.

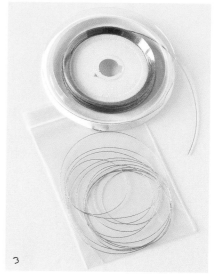

FINDINGS

This is the term for the various elements and accessories that set off and finish jewelry projects. They are the essential complement to many creations.

CLASPS (1)

There are many kinds of clasps (silver, gold, or copper) that can be adapted to the style, size, and weight of the project you are making. Screw or barrel clasps are used mainly for necklaces. Spring rings and lobster-claws are easy to attach and suitable for most jewelry, as they are anchored by jump rings. You can also make your own fastening with a loop on one side and a bobble of beads on the other, or by simply tying ribbons together.

CRIMP BEADS (2)

These tiny metallic beads are used to stop a bead or to fix thread that cannot be knotted, such as soft-flex wire. Crimp beads are discreet and practical, and come in a variety of sizes and finishes.

KNOT COVERS AND CRIMP-ENDS (3)

As their name indicates, knot covers, or bead tips, are used to cover a wire or ribbon knot. To fix them in place, put a dab of glue inside the covers before closing them around the knot. There are two basic types of knot covers—single cup-shaped and double clamshell-shaped—that come in different sizes, colors, and finishes.

Ribbon crimp-ends are flat closures that neatly finish the ends of ribbon used for chokers and bracelets. To use, simply fold over the end of the ribbon and firmly close the crimp-end over it.

JUMP RINGS (4)

Gold- or silver-colored jump rings come in several sizes. They are used to join two elements together or to extend a clasp. To open a jump ring, hold it with 2 flat-nose pliers, one on each side. Twist the ring gently to open without damaging it, drawing one side toward you and pushing the other side in the opposite direction. To close the ring, reverse the procedure, again using the 2 pliers.

EYE PINS AND HEAD PINS (5)

These are metal pins with either an eye-hole or a flat head on the tip. They are quite flexible and can be easily cut with wire cutters to the desired length and worked into a hoop or loop. They come in gold, silver, or copper finishes.

PIN AND RING MOUNTINGS (6)

These mountings both come in two parts. A pin mounting is a flat perforated template fixed to a base-plate with a pin on the back. Ring mountings use a perforated base fixed to a ring shape. There are also ring mountings with one or more sockets, and for bracelets, there are coils of memory wire that look like a spring.

NECK RINGS (7)

These are rigid silver- or gold-plated hoops made from memory wire. Use them to hang charms or pendants. Smaller versions can be used to make bracelets.

1

6

4

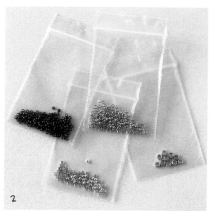

2

6

6

3

7

6

6

3

6

ADDITIONAL DECORATIONS

Specialist craft shops are full of many kinds of ornaments. Search around and improvise from all the treasures you discover.

Rhinestones (1) in a variety of shapes, simple or sophisticated drops and pendants (2), glass or plastic sequins and spangles (3), paillettes (4) of different diameters, cabochons (5), and feathers all lend themselves to many different effects.
Buttons (6) are indispensable, and can be used in a variety of projects. Rummage for buttons in notion stores, thrift shops, or garage sales: you might unearth unusual finds to create modern and original jewelry.
Ribbons and cords, available from textile stores, are useful for varying bases and for making necklaces and bracelets. Choose ribbons from a wide range of materials—real or imitation leather, satin, velvet, organza, and jacquard—which can all be adapted to fit many kinds of ornaments.

BEFORE YOU BEGIN

Instructions for making all the projects in this book are explained with step-by-step illustrations and detailed drawings. You can vary the combinations of materials and colors that we suggest, but before you begin, here are several things to bear in mind.

• When making jewelry, it is important to be seated comfortably and in good light.
• Keep a mirror nearby to try on work as it is made.
• Put everything needed on a large tray to collect the beads easily if they spill. This will also enable work to be set aside quickly if interrupted.
• Upturned jar lids are useful for sorting beads and managing them easily.

MEASUREMENTS

One of the pleasures of handmade jewelry is being able to adapt it to your size or that of your friends. Here are some standard lengths that will help to customize jewelry projects.

Ring: $2^1/_2$–3 in (6–8 cm)
Bracelet: approx. 7 in (18 cm)
Choker: approx. 14 in (36 cm)
Single-strand necklace: 20–24 in (50–60 cm)
Sautoir (long chain necklace): 32 in (80 cm) to 10 ft (3 m)

There are two easy ways to find the exact size of a finger: use a tape-measure to find the diameter in inches, or simply wrap a piece of paper around the finger and mark the exact size with a pencil.

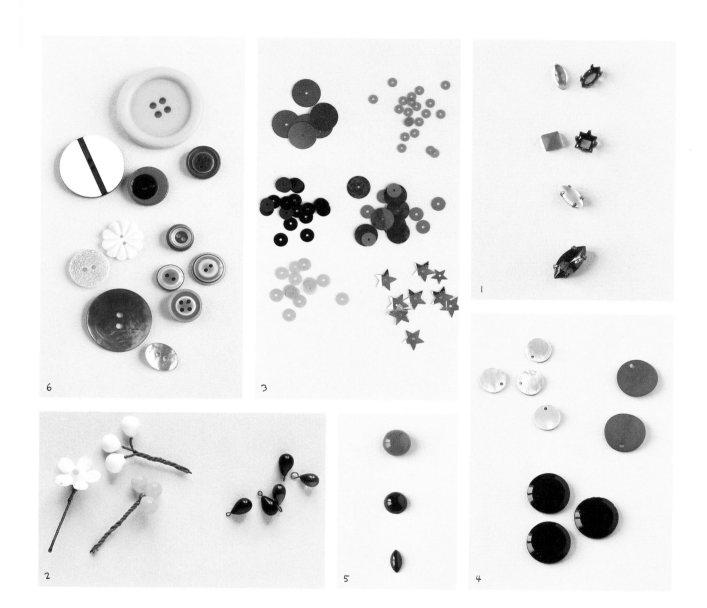

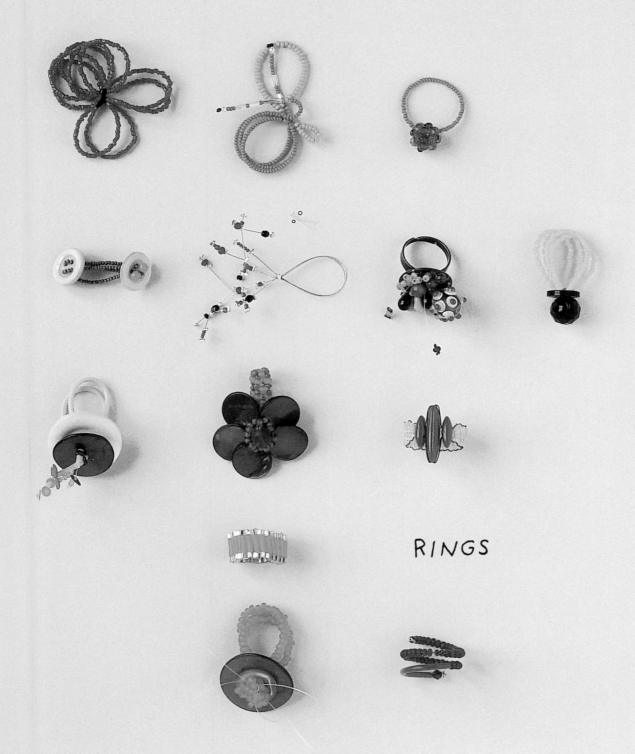

RINGS

BULL'S-EYE, instructions page 20

GLASS FLOWER, instructions page 22

BULL'S EYE

A simple, pretty button can be transformed into something beautiful. The clever way this button is combined with plastic lacing gives it a quirky, minimalist touch.

MATERIALS

- 4 in (10 cm) white plastic lacing (see page 9)
- 1 red, white, and blue plastic button (approx. 1 in/25 mm in diameter) with two holes large enough to thread the lacing through
- scissors

1 Make a tight knot at one end of the lacing. Trim off the lacing close to the knot, and pull the other end through one of the buttonholes.

2 Take the lacing up through the other buttonhole, leaving behind a length of lacing to fit around your finger. Tie off the lacing at the top of the button and trim close to the knot.

VARIATIONS

You can make this ring using all sorts of two-holed buttons. Choose the color of the plastic lacing to complement the color of your selected button: either to match or contrast with it.

I

2

TWIST

The charm and elegance of this simply colored ring comes from alternating the finishes with different beads.

MATERIALS

• 1 silver ring hoop made from memory wire, with several hoops
• 2 small, silver crimp beads
• 1 red crystal bicone (4 mm)
• a few inches of red plastic lacing (see page 9)
• 44 red matte transparent seed beads (8/0)
• 6 red, shiny transparent seed beads (11/0)
• 4 red opaque seed beads (8/0)
• flat-nose pliers

1 Put a crimp bead on one end of the ring hoop and crimp it with flat-nose pliers.

2 Thread on the red crystal, followed by around 1⅜ in (3.5 cm) of plastic lacing. Thread on the other beads until you reach the end of the ring-hoop, placing them in the following order:
8 matte transparent beads, 2 shiny transparent beads, 9 matte transparent beads, 2 opaque beads, 9 matte transparent beads, 2 shiny transparent beads, 9 matte transparent beads, 2 opaque beads, 9 matte transparent beads, and 2 shiny transparent beads.

3 Finish by threading on a crimp bead and crimping it.

HINT

Make sure to select seed beads with a center diameter large enough to push through the ring hoop, which is quite inflexible.

VARIATIONS

You could create a two-colored effect by carefully alternating the beads—try purple and yellow or blue and black.

You can also buy bracelet-hoops, which can be worked in the same way.

1

2

GLASS FLOWER

Covering the whole finger, this impressive, flat ring is a mixture of modern and traditional.
The combination of colors, shapes, and materials gives it a chic, art deco look.

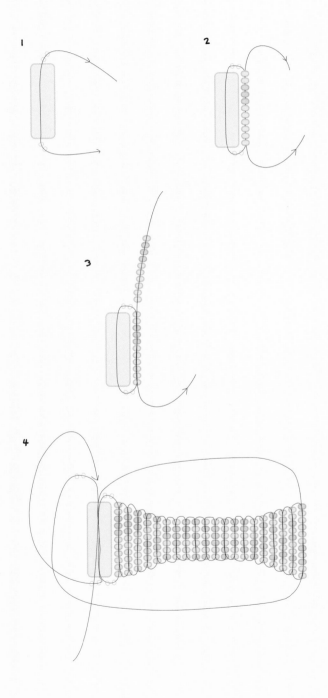

MATERIALS

- approx. 1⅓ yds (1.2 m) gold-tone jewelry wire (28 gauge)
- 1 molded glass bead with a floral motif (around 20 mm x 7 mm)
- 8 white pearl seed beads (15/0)
- approx. 110 pale-green matte seed beads (8/0)
- approx. 40 pale-green pearl seed beads (8/0)
- wire cutters
- quick-drying glue

1 Thread the molded glass bead onto the jewelry wire. Push it to the center, then fold the wire in half. Add 2 white pearl beads to each end of the wire.

2 Calculate the number of seed beads needed to make the first row of the ring by measuring the length of the glass bead. As the one photographed is around 20 mm long (see page 18), the first row of seed beads calls for 11 green beads (matte and pearl). Thread the beads onto one end of the wire and pass the other end through all the beads, crossing the wires to make 1 row.

3 Make the other rows of the ring, shortening their length progressively. Work carefully, making sure to alternate the matte and pearl beads, to this pattern:

1 row of 10 seed beads; 1 row of 9 seed beads;
1 row of 8 seed beads; 1 row of 7 seed beads;
10 rows of 6 seed beads (middle of the ring, adjust number of rows to fit your finger);
1 row of 7 seed beads; 1 row of 8 seed beads;
1 row of 9 seed beads; 1 row of 10 seed beads;
1 row of 11 seed beads.

4 When you have completed all the rows, add 2 white pearl seed beads to each end of the wire. Draw each end of the wire through the glass bead, then pass the wire several times through the rows surrounding the glass bead. Cut the wire short and add a dab of glue to consolidate the closure. Allow to dry, then trim off with wire cutters.

HINT

It's the way that different types of beads (matte and pearl, or opaque and transparent) alternate in each row that gives this ring its luster and its own personality. You can also add a white pearl seed bead to the end of each row (see photograph, page 18).

RAZZLE-DAZZLE

Oblong shapes, bright colors, and black jewelry wire that isn't ashamed to be on display make this ring a faux-classical jewel—like a rather eccentric marquise.

MATERIALS

- approx. 1⅓ yds (1.2 m) black jewelry wire (28 gauge)
- 2 red, oblong glass beads, each 13 mm long (with two holes on each side)
- 1 green, oblong plastic bead, 22 mm long
- approx. 80 bright-yellow matte seed beads (13/0)
- approx. 60 yellow luster seed beads (13/0)
- wire cutters
- quick-drying glue

1 String 1 red bead onto the jewelry wire, passing each end of the wire through a separate hole. Center the bead on the wire and pull the ends straight. Thread the green bead onto one end of the wire. Push the other end of the wire through the bead, crossing the two wires. Tighten to fasten the green bead.

2 Add the second red bead to the wire, drawing each end through a separate hole. Add 3 bright-yellow seed beads and 1 yellow luster seed bead to one end of the wire. Draw the other end of the wire through these last 4 beads. Pull on the wires to obtain a row. Continue the band, alternating the bright-yellow beads with the luster beads, with 1 row of 5 beads, 20 rows of 6 beads, 1 row of 5 beads, and 1 row of 4 beads.

3 To finish, pass the wire through the red bead, bringing together the two ends of the ring. Pass the wires through the central green bead. Pull tight, and finish by pushing the wire through the second red bead. Add a drop of glue to secure. Allow to dry, and trim the wire closely with wire cutters.

VARIATIONS

This ring is very quick to make. You could use a rhinestone pierced at both ends as the central feature. Bugle beads would also create a very pretty effect.

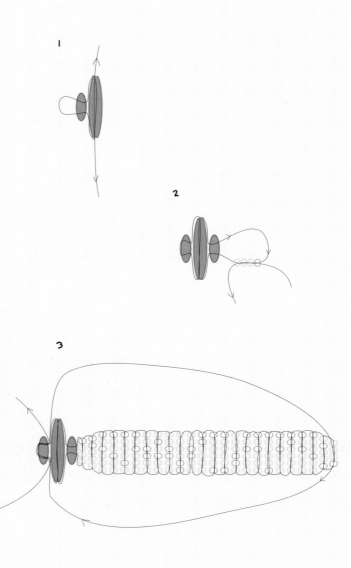

BLING RING, instructions page 28

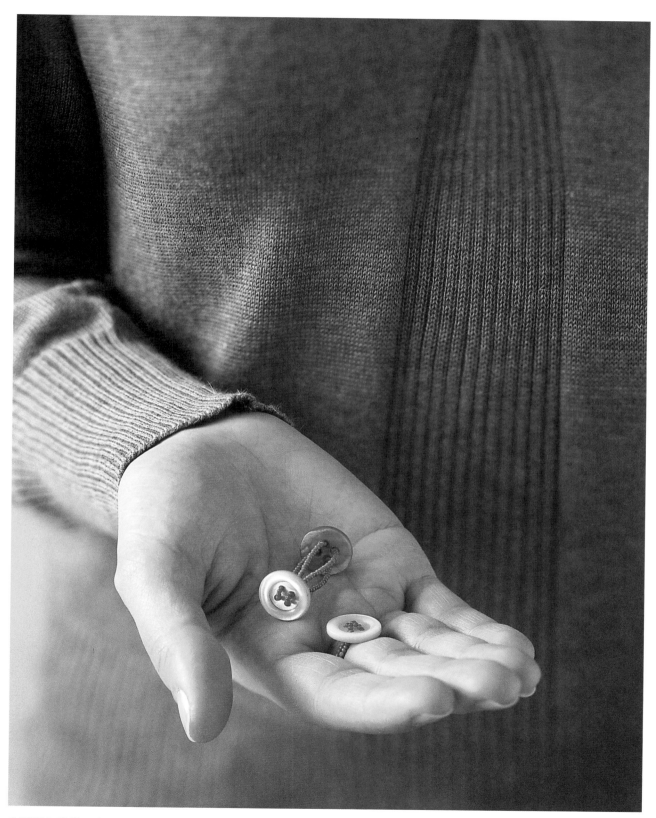

TOPSY-TURVY, instructions page 29

SMALL AND SWEET, instructions page 30

MAGIC GARDEN, instructions page 31

BLING RING

In this design, a striking central bead is surrounded with a setting of little pearly beads. This ring is quickly made and the antique-style cabochon has a dazzling effect.

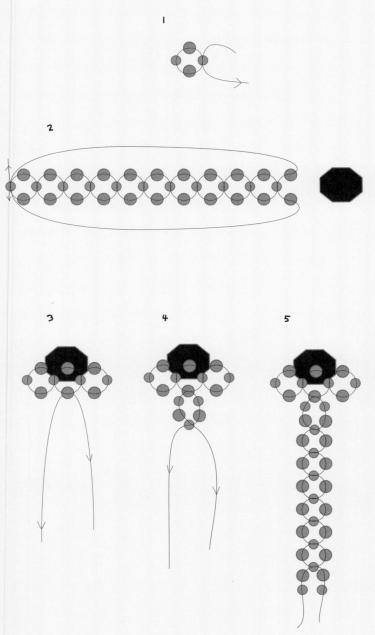

MATERIALS

- 2¼ yds (2 m) black jewelry wire (28 gauge)
- approx. 23 silver, round beads (3 mm)
- approx. 38 violet, pearly, round beads (4 mm)
- 1 large, black opaque faceted bead (15 mm)
- wire cutters

1 Cut the jewelry wire in half with wire cutters. Thread 1 silver bead, 1 violet bead, 1 silver bead, and 1 violet bead onto 1 strand of wire. Fold the wire in half and push one end of the wire through the last silver bead to make a loop. Thread 1 violet bead onto each end of the wire, then thread 1 silver bead onto one end only. Pass the other end through the silver bead to form a second loop. Repeat this operation eight times.

2 When you have made the tenth and last loop, thread 1 violet bead onto each end of the wire, then cross the wires through the first silver bead to make a circlet. Thread the 2 wires through the large black bead, then pull the wires through the beads on the other side of the circlet. Adjust the large bead in the center of the circlet. Close by pulling the wires through the pearly beads several times, then trim off.

3 Thread the second length of wire onto one of the violet beads on the lower row of the ring and center it. Fold the wire on the lower row in half.

4 Thread 1 silver and 1 violet bead onto each end of the wire. Thread another silver bead onto one end only, then pass the other end through the bead to form a loop.

5 Continue making the band by threading 1 violet bead onto each end of the wire and then threading both ends through 1 silver bead until you have made as many loops as necessary to fit your finger. When you have made the final loop, thread 1 violet bead and 1 silver bead onto each wire. Close the band by passing the wires into the opposite side of the ring and pulling them through the beads several times. Trim off with wire cutters.

VARIATION

Use the same method to make a bracelet: repeat the central cabochon made from the circlet and the large faceted bead 3 or 4 times and place the loops in between.

TOPSY-TURVY

Yin or Yang. Up or down. This two-faced ring has a dual personality. Whichever side you decide to show, the other won't be revealed until you turn over your hand...

MATERIALS

- 20 in (50 cm) nylon thread (size 0)
- 1 small, pale-green 4-hole mother-of-pearl button (1/2 in/12 mm in diameter)
- 1 small, red 4-hole mother-of-pearl button (1/2 in/12 mm in diameter)
- 8 red opaque seed beads (15/0)
- approx. 100 mauve opaque seed beads (15/0)
- 8 purple opaque seed beads (11/0)
- scissors
- quick-drying glue

1 String 4 red seed beads on the nylon thread. Fold the thread in half and pull each end through two of the holes in 1 button.

2 Depending on the size of your finger, string approximately 24 mauve seed beads on each end of the thread, finishing with 1 purple seed bead on each end.

3 Take each end of the thread through two holes in the second button. String 4 red seed beads onto each end. Pull the threads back through the two empty buttonholes. You will have 2 rows of beads, side by side, on top of the button. This side of the ring is now complete.

4 String 24 mauve seed beads on each side of the thread, then add 1 purple seed bead to each end. Take the threads through the empty buttonholes of the second button. Add 4 red seed beads to one thread and pull it through the opposite buttonhole to make a cross on the top of the button. Then take the other end of the thread through the opposite buttonhole, knot the 2 threads together, and glue to secure before trimming off.

HINT

Two of these funky rings can be used as cufflinks. Simply reduce the number of beads between the two buttons to obtain the correct size.

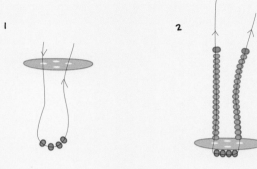

1

2

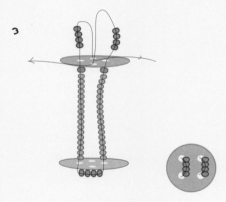

3

4

SMALL AND SWEET

It only takes a few seed beads to make this little circlet of flowers, which has the rustic simplicity of a daisy chain in springtime.

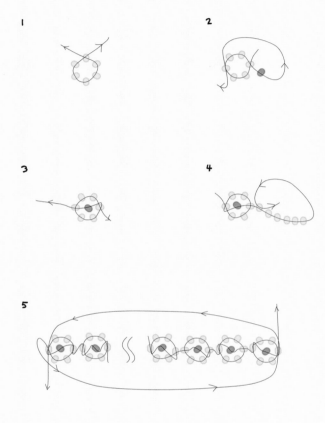

MATERIALS (for the pink version)
• 18 in (45 cm) gold-tone jewelry wire (28 gauge)
• approx. 60 pink-lined crystal seed beads (15/0)
• approx. 10 red opaque seed beads (15/0)
• wire cutters

1 String 6 pink beads onto the wire and place them in the center. Fold the wire in half and pass one end back through the first bead to form a loop. Tug the wire to tighten the loop and create a circle of petals.

2 Add 1 red bead to one end of the wire then take the tip of this wire through the bead opposite.

3 Pull the wire to draw the red bead into the center of the flower. Adjust if necessary.

4 Add another 6 pink beads and follow steps 1–3 to make a second flower. Repeat until you have made the required number of flowers.

5 To finish, make into a ring shape by bringing the two ends together. Link the ends by threading each end of the wire through a bead on the other side. Pull the wires through several other beads to secure the fastening, then trim off with wire cutters.

MAGIC GARDEN

With its sparkly branches of tiny beads and sequins, this unusual ring could represent an exotic flower or a fantasy garden.

MATERIALS

- 24 in (60 cm) nylon thread (size 0)
- approx. 8 in (20 cm) purple plastic lacing for the ring (see page 9) + 1 in (25 mm) for decoration
- 1 white 4-hole mother-of-pearl button (1⅛ in/28 mm in diameter)
- 1 bright-pink 2-hole mother-of-pearl button (⅞ in/22 mm in diameter)
- 2 large, silver crimp beads
- 4 pink matte opaque seed beads (13/0)
- 3 small, fluorescent-pink transparent sequins (3/16 in/4 mm)
- 2 large, bright-pink, sparkling sequins (3/8 in/10 mm)
- scissors
- flat-nose pliers
- quick-drying glue

I Cut the nylon thread in half. Draw both pieces through the plastic lacing to stiffen it.

2 Push one end of the lacing through one of the holes in the white button, then pass it back through the hole diagonally opposite. Draw the button to the middle of the wire.

3 Take each end of the lacing through one of the two empty holes, adjusting the two resulting loops to fit your finger.

4 Place the bright-pink button on the top of the ring and thread each end of the lacing through one of the buttonholes.

5 Put a crimp bead on each piece of lacing and push down onto the bright-pink button. Crimp together with flat-nose pliers. The basic structure is now complete: two nylon threads should stick out from each branch (A and B) of plastic lacing. Now you can add decorations to the two threads on each branch.

Branch A. Make a double knot in one of the nylon threads. Thread on 3 seed beads and make another double knot. On the other thread, make a double knot, thread on 1 large sequin (shape it into a flower shape with sharp scissors or leave it as is), 1/16 in (2 mm) of plastic lacing, and 1 seed bead. Make a double knot.

Branch B. Thread both nylon threads through 1 large sequin (snipped into a flower shape with sharp scissors). Knot the two threads together. On one thread, place 1 small sequin, 1/8 in (3 mm) of plastic lacing, and another small sequin, then make a double knot. Leave the other piece of thread slightly longer and tie a knot. Thread on 1 small sequin, then make a double knot. Add a dot of glue to each knot, allow to dry, and trim the thread.

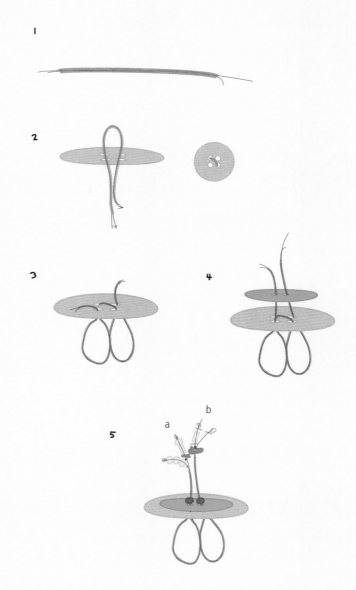

VARIATION

You could make a simple version of this ring by just knotting the ends of the plastic lacing. In this case, there is no need to push the nylon thread through it.

OPERA, instructions page 34

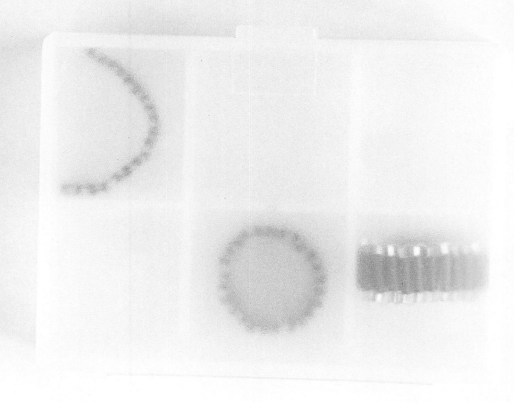

FASCINATING RHYTHM, instructions page 35

OPERA

This elegant black ring reflects light from its many facets.
Wear it during the daytime to remind you of a night at the opera.

1

2

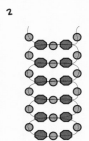

3

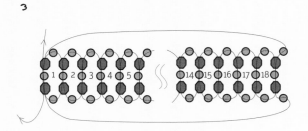

MATERIALS (for the black version)

• 24 in (60 cm) black jewelry wire (30 gauge)
• approx. 40 black matte seed beads (11/0)
• approx. 40 black faceted Czech glass beads (3 mm)
• wire cutters

1 String onto the jewelry wire: 1 seed bead, 1 faceted bead, 1 seed bead, 1 faceted bead, then another seed bead. Place the beads in the center of the wire, then fold it in half. Add 1 faceted bead, 1 seed bead, and another faceted bead to one end of the wire, then take the other end of the wire through each of these last 3 beads.

2 Tighten the wire and adjust to obtain 2 rows. Add 1 seed bead to one end of the wire. String onto the other end: 1 seed bead, 1 faceted bead, 1 seed bead, then another faceted bead. Pass the first end of the wire through the last 3 beads. Tighten the wire to obtain another row. Continue in this way until you reach the desired length.

3 To finish, make the ring shape by bringing the two ends together. Thread 1 seed bead onto each end. Pull each wire through the beads on the first row of the ring, and consolidate the closure by taking the wire back through several other rows of beads. Trim the wire with wire cutters.

HINT

This method can be used to make more sophisticated jewelry, like the elegant bracelet on page 138 (Night Music).

FASCINATING RHYTHM

This discreet and elegant ring wraps comfortably around the finger.
It's as easily adapted to your mood as to the size of your finger.

MATERIALS

- 39 in (1 m) gold-tone jewelry wire (28 gauge)
- approx. 60 pale-pink and orange bugle beads (7 mm)
- round-nose pliers
- wire cutters

1 Thread 2 pink and 2 orange bugle beads onto the wire and push
them to the center.

2 Fold the wire in half to create 2 rows of 2 beads and 2 wire
ends. Take one end of the wire through the 2 beads on the upper
row. Pull the wire tight to adjust the rows of beads.

3 Add 2 pink beads to one end of the wire. Fold the wire, then
pass the other end through each of these beads. Repeat this weave
until you reach the correct length to encircle your finger, varying
the colors to your own design.

4 Finish the ring by bringing the two sides together. Cross each
wire through the first row of beads opposite. Pull tight, using
round-nose pliers. To secure the ring, pass the wire once or twice
through the other rows of beads. Trim the wire with wire cutters.

VARIATIONS

Select beads in contrasting colors for the ring, using them in
whatever order you prefer.

This method can be used with other types of beads, such as seed
beads, which can be combined with bugle beads. Or you could work
with longer beads, alternating with a row of seed beads.

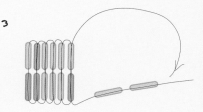

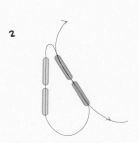

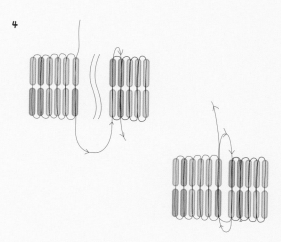

SUNFLOWER

Think of all those buttons languishing unused in your sewing box, and make this pretty
sunflower to flourish on your finger. It's a simple project made from practically nothing.

MATERIALS

• 1 flat-topped ring mounting ($^3/_8$ in/10 mm in diameter)
• 1 black, glass or plastic cabochon (8 mm)
• 1 flower-shaped mother-of-pearl button (1 in/25 mm in diameter)
• slow-drying glue

1 Glue the black cabochon to the middle of the pearl button.

2 Glue the whole ensemble on the ring-mount. Allow to dry.

HINTS

When positioning the cabochon, play around with the central holes
of the big button that forms the base of the design. You can decide
whether to let all or some of them show.

You can make this ring from a variety of buttons and flat-backed
beads. Let your imagination run riot.

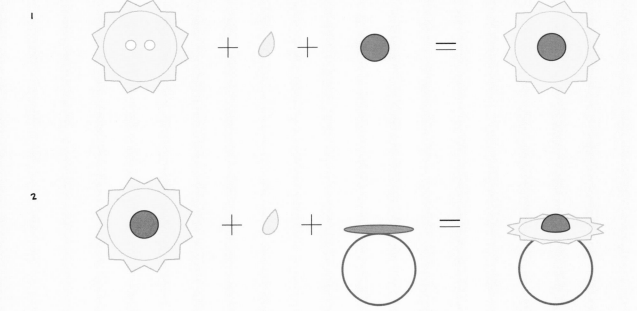

CLEAR WINNER, instructions page 40

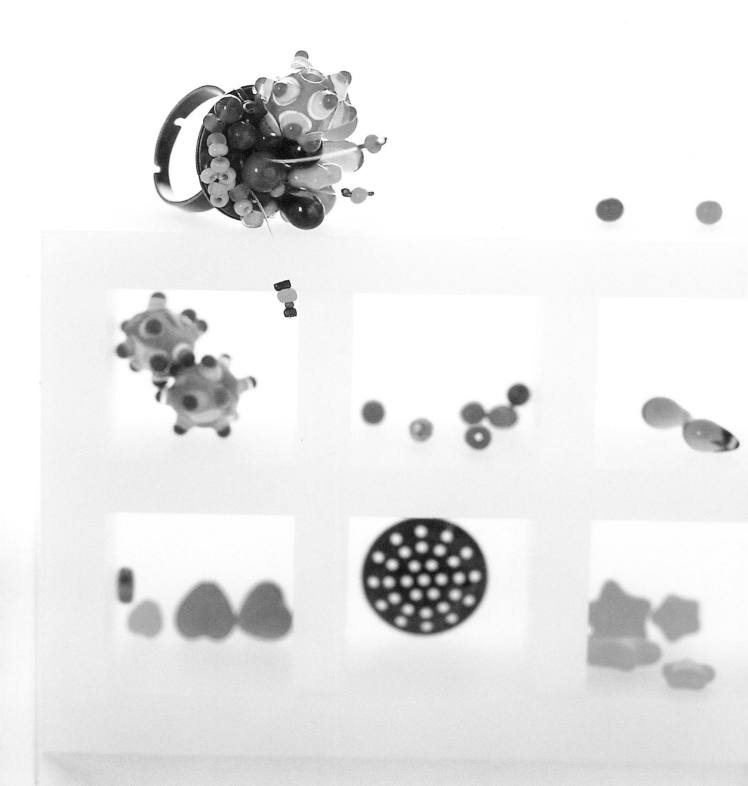

CENTER STAGE, instructions page 41

CLEAR WINNER

Light, colorless, and stiff, nylon thread is transformed into a sparkling ornament—almost invisible yet very evident, this ring makes a cheeky and lighthearted silhouette.

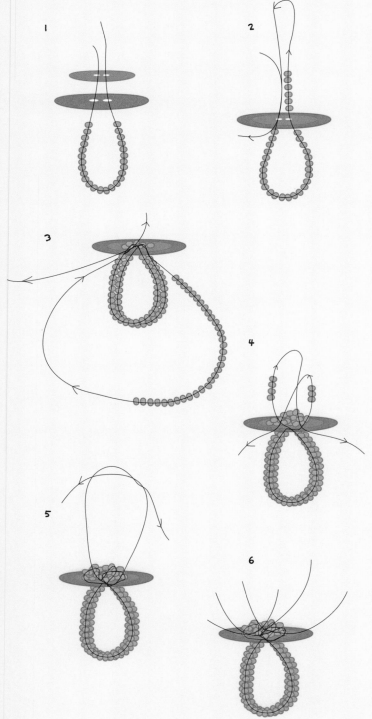

MATERIALS (for the red version)

- 32 in (80 cm) nylon thread (size 0)
- approx. 130-150 orange matte transparent seed beads (9/0)
- 1 large, red 2-hole mother-of-pearl button (1 in/25 mm in diameter)
- 1 small, red 2-hole mother-of-pearl button (5/8 in/15 mm in diameter)
- scissors
- quick-drying glue

1 Using 24 in (60 cm) of nylon thread, string on enough seed beads to make a ring to fit your finger (approximately 30 beads). Fold the thread in half. Take each end of the thread through one of the holes in the large button, then through one of the holes in the small one.

2 Thread 6 seed beads onto one end and take the thread through the second hole in each button. Repeat with the other end of the nylon thread, but this time add 4 beads to the thread.

3 Slide onto one end of the thread enough seed beads to make a second loop the size of your finger (approximately 30 beads). Take the thread through one of the holes in each button. Proceed in the same manner with the other thread. You will now have 3 loops of seed beads and the tips of the thread should stick out from the small button.

4 Add 3 beads to one end of the thread, then add 4 beads to the other and arrange them in the center of the small button. Repeat this operation as many times as you wish until the center of the button is more or less filled with beads.

5 Pass the threads through the small button and knot them, then trim off, leaving ³/₄–1¹/₂ in (2–4 cm) sticking out on each side.

6 Finish by adding short lengths of nylon thread to the top of the ring. Use two 4 in- (10 cm-) lengths, knot them around the beads and trim to the desired length.

VARIATION

You can also make this ring without its little nylon "whiskers".

CENTER STAGE

This ring can tell a story or present a scene. The mount is like the set on a tiny stage...
now it's your turn to play.

MATERIALS

• approx. 1½ yds (1.3 m) nylon thread (size 0)
• 1 copper ring mounting (¾ in/20 mm in diameter)
• 1 red, flat, heart-shaped glass bead
• 1 orange-yellow, star-shaped glass bead
• 1 red, round transparent glass bead (4 mm)
• 1 red, round opaque glass bead (4 mm)
• 1 blue lampwork glass bead, decorated with red spots (see page 6)
• 3 small, blue transparent glass drops
• 4 red, round transparent glass beads (2 mm)
• 10–12 small, copper crimp beads
• 10 orange matte transparent seed beads (11/0)
• 10 pale-blue matte transparent seed beads (11/0)
• 10 yellow seed beads (11/0)
• flat-nose pliers
• scissors
• small spoon

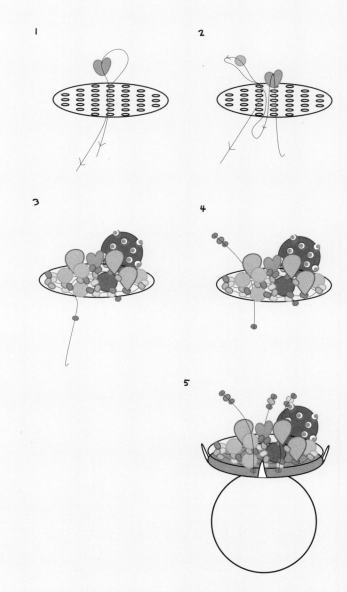

1 Cut a 39 in- (1 m-) length of nylon thread and use it to attach
the beads to the ring mounting—the heart, the round beads, the
large glass bead with the red spots, the glass drops, etc.—until a
pleasing composition is achieved. Finish by attaching a crimp bead
to the threads under the mount and crimp it with flat-nose pliers.
Trim the thread.

2 Cut a 12 in- (30 cm-) length of nylon thread and string onto it
some orange, blue, and yellow seed beads to wind through the
arrangement and hide any holes. Allow 7–8 beads of each color.

3 Finish off by adding a crimp bead under the mount, and crimp
it. Trim the thread.

4 To make the filaments, cut 3 pieces of nylon thread to 1½,
1¼ and ¾ in (4, 3 and 2 cm) lengths. Place 1 crimp bead on the tip
of the longest thread and crimp. Take the thread through the
mount from below, wedging the crimp bead on the underside.
Crimp another crimp bead ¼ in (5 mm) on the other end. Thread
on 1 pale-blue seed bead. Add another crimp bead. Trim the excess
thread. Repeat the operation with the second length of thread:
1 crimp bead placed under the mount and another crimp bead
placed ¼ in (5 mm) from the end of the thread. String 1 orange
seed bead onto the thread. Add a last crimp bead. Trim the excess
thread. Repeat this step with the shortest length of thread, using
1 yellow seed bead and 3 crimp beads.

5 Position the mount on the ring structure and close the claws
with the help of a small spoon.

VARIATION

You could simply decorate the ring mount by supplementing the
filaments with seed beads.

MARQUISE, instructions pages 44–45

LACE, instructions pages 46–47

MARQUISE

This sophisticated ring adds a dash of novelty to a traditional form. The central ornament brings it up to date, while its milky whiteness adds a touch of class.

MATERIALS

- 2 yds (1.8 m) nylon beading thread (size 0)
- approx. 24 chalk-white faceted beads (4 mm)
- approx. 66 chalk-white faceted beads (3 mm)
- approx. 18 milky-white crystal bicones (3 mm)
- approx. 17 white transparent crystal bicones (3 mm)
- 2 milky-white crystal bicones (6 mm)
- 1 almond-green, oval glass bead (15 mm long)
- scissors
- quick-drying glue

This ring is composed of 2 chains that are made separately, and then assembled by attaching the central bead.

The chains

1 Begin by making a chain. Working with 24 in (60 cm) of nylon thread, string on a 4 mm-faceted bead, a 3 mm-faceted bead, a 4 mm-faceted bead, and a 3 mm-faceted bead. Pass one end of the thread through the first 4 mm-faceted bead to make a loop.

2 At one end of the nylon thread, string on a 3 mm-faceted bead, a milky-white crystal, a 3 mm-faceted bead, and a 4 mm-faceted bead. At the other end, thread on a 3 mm-faceted bead, then take this thread back through the last faceted bead on the other thread to make a loop. Repeat this step twice more to make 3 loops.

3 Make 3 more loops in the same fashion, but this time thread the crystal bicone onto the second thread, so that these loops appear upside down in relation to the first 3 loops. Make an additional 3 loops, placing the crystal in the same position as in the 3 loops in step 2. To finish, make a small loop in the following sequence: a 3 mm-faceted bead, a 4 mm-faceted bead, and a 3 mm-faceted bead. Then make a final loop using two 3 mm-faceted beads. Take the two ends through the first 4 mm-faceted bead to make a circle. Knot the threads. Add a drop of glue to the knot and allow to dry. Trim the thread. Make a second chain, following the same instructions.

THE CHAINS

1

2

3

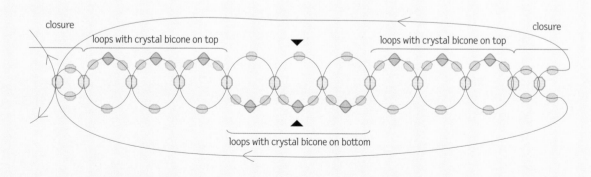

closure   loops with crystal bicone on top   loops with crystal bicone on top   closure

loops with crystal bicone on bottom

VARIATIONS

To make a less bulky ring, select a smaller central bead or perhaps just a simple round or baguette bead. The marquise shape can also be made into a pin. All you have to do is flatten the ring by drawing the threads of the chain through the structure and attach a pin mounting with nylon thread.

Assembly

1 Fold chain A in half to find the 4 mm-faceted bead that is exactly in the center. Draw a 24 in- (60 cm-) nylon thread through this bead and double over. Then thread both ends through one of the 6 mm-crystals, the oval green bead, and the second 6 mm-crystal. Cross the threads through the 4 mm-faceted bead in the middle of chain B. You will now have two ends of thread, which will be woven into the mesh that unites the two chains.

2 Working first on one side then on the other, take the thread through the two 3 mm-beads of chain B. Thread on four 3 mm-transparent crystals, then take the same thread through the milky-white crystal of chain A.

3 Draw this thread through the two 3 mm-faceted beads, then the milky-white crystal. Thread on two 3 mm-white transparent crystals and draw the thread through the milky-white crystal of the next loop on chain B.

4 Finish the thread by pulling it back through the same crystal, then through the two 3 mm-faceted beads. Add 1 transparent white crystal, then take the thread through the crystal in chain A.

5 Finish the thread by taking it back through the same crystal. Complete the other side of the ring in the same way with another 24 in- (60 cm-) thread. To finish, cross the 2 threads through the same 3 mm-faceted bead in the center of the chain and string 3 transparent white crystals on both threads. Then cross the 2 threads through the 3 mm-faceted bead of chain B. Pull the threads to tighten, and knot twice. Add a drop of glue, allow to dry, then trim the thread closely.

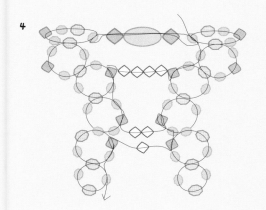

ASSEMBLY

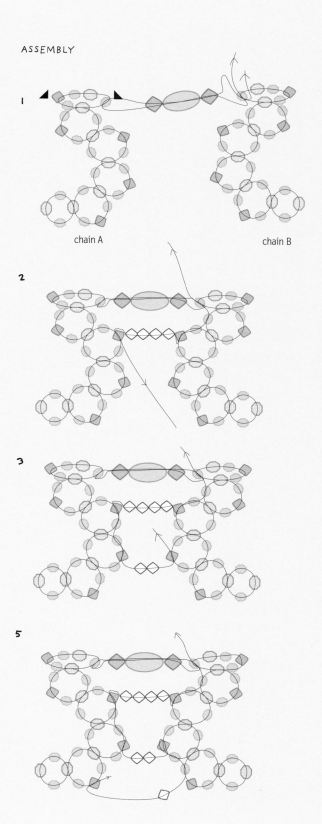

chain A   chain B

LACE

Whether you choose pastel or bold colors, the pretty lattice of this ring will dress up your finger in a lacework of beads.

MOTIF 1

1   2

MOTIF 2

1

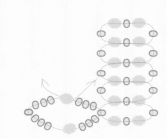

2

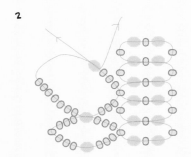

MATERIALS

Motif 1 (center)
- approx. 8 in (20 cm) gold-tone jewelry wire (28 gauge)
- 12 transparent crystal faceted beads (3 mm)
- 16 cream, pearl luster seed beads (11/0)
- wire cutters

Motif 2 (sides)
- approx. 39 in (1 m) gold-tone jewelry wire (30 gauge)
- 8 transparent crystal faceted beads (3 mm)
- 78 cream, pearl luster seed beads (11/0)
- wire cutters

Motif 3 (back)
- approx. 12 in (30 cm) gold-tone jewelry wire (28 gauge)
- 4 transparent crystal faceted beads (3 mm)
- approx. 60 cream, pearl luster seed beads (11/0)
- wire cutters

Motif 1 (center)

1 String 1 faceted bead, 1 seed bead, and 1 faceted bead onto the jewelry wire. Slide them to the center and fold the wire in half.

2 Add 1 seed bead to each end of the wire, then add 1 faceted bead, 1 seed bead, and a final faceted bead to one end of the wire. Take the other end through these 3 beads. Fold the wire to make 2 rows of beads. Repeat the operation until you have made 6 rows. Take the 2 wires back through the loops several times, crossing them to consolidate the closure. Trim the wire with wire cutters.

Motif 2 (sides)

1 Cut the wire into 2 equal pieces. With the underside of the central motif facing you, thread 1 piece of wire through the pearl seed bead at the base of the motif. Draw the wire through to the center of the bead to obtain 2 equal lengths. On the upper wire, string 3 seed beads and 1 faceted bead. On the lower wire, thread 3 seed beads, 1 faceted bead, and 7 seed beads. Cross this wire through the faceted bead on the upper wire. Gently fold the wire to create 2 identical rows of beads.

2 Continue weaving like this, working along the left side of Motif 1 and passing the wire through every second pearl bead, until you have made 3 loops. Take the wires through the loops several times, crossing them to consolidate the closure. Trim off. Repeat Motif 2 along the right side of Motif 1 using the second piece of wire.

Motif 3 (back)

I Complete the ring by making Motif 3 in the same fashion as
Motif 2, varying the length by adding extra seed beads to fit your
finger. To finish, pass the wires through the loops several times,
crossing them to consolidate the closure. Trim off.

HINT

This ring can be worn in two ways: you can display the central
motif on the top of your finger or slide it round to reveal a more
discreet look.

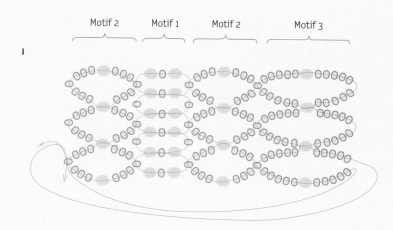

MOTIF 3

Motif 2   Motif 1   Motif 2   Motif 3

I

LITTLE BELLS, instructions page 50

TREE OF LIFE, instructions page 51

LITTLE BELLS

"Rings on her fingers, bells on her toes ..."
With these little charms tinkling on your finger, you'll have music wherever you go.

MATERIALS

- 1 ring hoop with a loop
- 1 small, copper jump ring (3 mm in diameter)
- 1 small, red bell
- 3 red crystal drops
- 1 large, copper jump ring (12 mm in diameter)
- 4 black opaque glass drops (with wire stems)
- 2 flat-nose pliers
- round-nose pliers

1 Open the small jump ring using 2 flat-nose pliers. Twist gently so as not to pull the ring out of shape, drawing one side toward you and the other side in the opposite direction. Place the bell on the jump ring and fix this to the loop of the ring hoop, closing the jump ring with the flat-nose pliers.

2 Attach the 3 red crystal drops to the large jump ring, opening it as described in step 1.

3 Using round-nose pliers, make a small loop in the stem of each of the black drops, and attach them to the 12 mm-jump ring. (If you cannot find drops with wire stems, buy some ordinary drops and affix them with head pins.)

4 Attach this jump ring to the ring hoop, passing it through the loop and the jump ring of the bell. Close the ring with flat-nose pliers.

VARIATION

You can use many different kinds of charms to decorate a ring hoop, which also come with multiple loops.

1

2

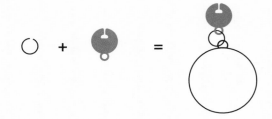

3

4

TREE OF LIFE

With its slender branches, this ring appears to grow on your finger.
The delicate but sturdy little bonsai will charm and intrigue everyone who sees it.

MATERIALS

- 12 in (30 cm) silver soft-flex wire for the ring
  + an extra 8 in (20 cm) for attaching elements
- 33 small, silver crimp beads
- 3 black opaque faceted beads (3 mm)
- 5 black matte transparent seed beads (11/0)
- 4 red matte transparent (large) seed beads (8/0)
- 8 red opaque (medium) seed beads (11/0)
- 13 red pearl (small) seed beads (15/0)
- flat-nose pliers
- wire cutters

1 Cut the long piece of wire into 3 equal pieces and fold each to make 3 loops the diameter of your finger. Put all 6 pieces of wire through a crimp bead and crimp with flat-nose pliers.

2 Spread out the 6 wires at the top of the loop, making 6 branches (a, b, c, d, e, f): each will be decorated in a different style.

3 String the beads onto each branch, following the 6 diagrams shown, being careful to add a crimp bead every time you add a supplementary wire or when you need to anchor a bead. Keep the shape of a tree in mind while you are working—you need to prepare the main branches before adding the extra elements.

The branches use the following beads:
a 5 crimp beads, 1 black faceted bead, 3 medium, red seed beads
b 14 crimp beads, 1 black faceted bead, 2 black seed beads, 2 large, red seed beads, 2 medium, red seed beads, 3 small, red seed beads
c 2 crimp beads, 2 medium, red seed beads
d 7 crimp beads, 1 black faceted bead, 2 large, red seed beads, 1 medium, red seed bead, 5 small, red seed beads
e 2 crimp beads, 5 small, red seed beads
f 2 crimp beads, 3 black seed beads

HINT

Like a tree, this design is structured from the bottom to the top. The branches can be as long as you wish. Shorter wires will make the ring easier to wear.

1

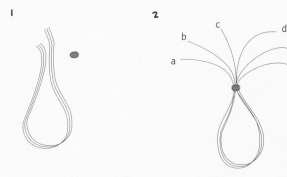

2

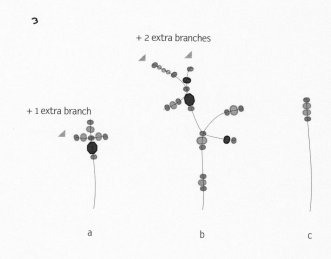

+ 2 extra branches

+ 1 extra branch

a   b   c

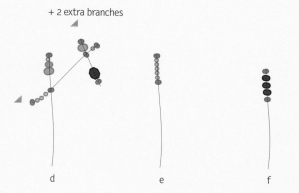

+ 2 extra branches

d   e   f

SOLAR ECLIPSE

Like the rays of the sun eclipsed by the moon, the facets of the solitaire bead light up this plain, elegant ring. The play of light and shade is enhanced by its simplicity.

MATERIALS

- 32 in (80 cm) nylon thread (size 0)
- approx. 176 yellow opaque seed beads (11/0)
- 1 black 4-hole button (½ in/12 mm in diameter)
- 1 black faceted glass bead (13 mm)
- scissors
- quick-drying glue

1 String approximately 44 seed beads onto the nylon thread and push them to the center. Double the thread to create a loop the size of your finger. If necessary, adjust the fit by adding or subtracting beads. Working with the two holes on one side of the button, take the two ends of the thread through two adjacent holes, then take each thread back through the opposite hole, so that the threads are underneath the button.

2 Working with one end of the thread, string on the same number of seed beads as in step 1. Pass the thread back through one of the buttonholes used to attach the first loop of beads, then draw it back through the other hole. You now have 2 loops of beads under the button.

3 Pass one end of the thread through the empty buttonhole diagonally opposite and follow the same procedure to make 2 more loops.

4 When you have made 4 loops, bring the threads up to the top of the button, through two diagonally opposite buttonholes. Cross each thread through opposite ends of the faceted bead, taking them back through the buttonholes so that they are underneath the ring, and make several knots. Add a dot of glue to the knots, allow to dry, and trim off.

HINT

You could wear only two loops on your finger and leave the other two on the top of your hand, surrounding the bead like the wings of a butterfly.

VARIATION

Vary the central bead as you wish. Just be careful to balance the proportions of the button (which acts as a socket) and the round bead. They should preferably be the same color with contrasting beads used to make the loops.

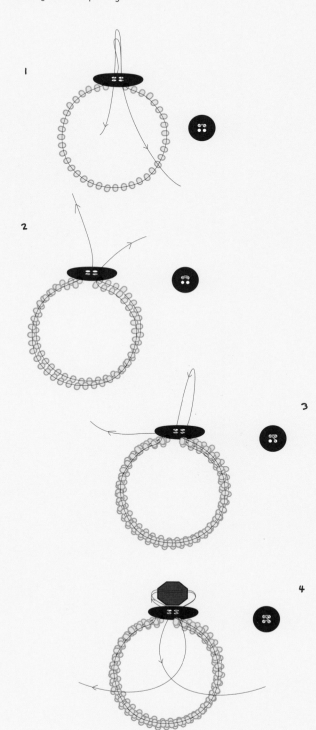

FLOWER POWER, instructions pages 56–57

POMPOM, instructions pages 58–59

FLOWER POWER

This flower with mother-of-pearl petals is unashamedly romantic with a real retro feel.
It displays a happy blend of materials and a hippy-chic appeal.

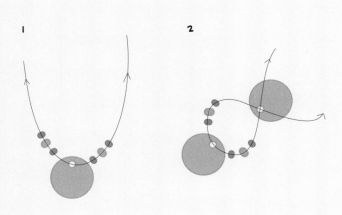

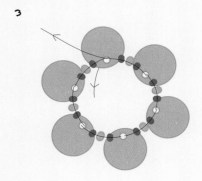

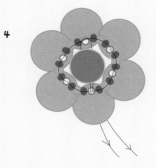

MATERIALS (for the red version)

For the flower
- 20 in (50 cm) nylon thread (size 0)
- 6 red, polished mother-of-pearl paillettes (15 mm)
- 12 coral-red matte opaque seed beads (13/0)
- 6 orange matte transparent seed beads (8/0)
- 1 large, coral-red bead (8 mm)
- scissors
- quick-drying glue

For the ring
- 16 in (40 cm) nylon thread (size 0)
- approx. 40 orange matte transparent seed beads (8/0)
- approx. 30 coral-red matte opaque seed beads (13/0)
- scissors
- quick-drying glue

To make the flower

1 Thread 1 paillette through to the middle of the 20 in- (50 cm-) nylon thread. String onto each end of the thread: 1 coral-red seed bead, 1 orange seed bead, and 1 coral-red seed bead.

2 Add a second paillette to one end of the thread. Take the other end of the thread through the same paillette, crossing the threads. Add 3 beads in the same sequence as in step 1 on top of each paillette, and 3 others similarly beneath.

3 Repeat step 2 until you have used all 6 paillettes, each time threading onto either end of the thread: 1 coral-red bead, 1 orange bead, and 1 coral-red bead. When you reach the last paillette, you will have 1 thread on top and 1 underneath. Draw the thread underneath through a seed bead to secure it and pull it around to the top.

4 Take both ends of the thread through the large, round coral bead, then draw these threads through the hole in the paillette opposite. The 2 threads should now be underneath the flower. To secure the threads, take 1 thread through all the beads underneath. Knot the threads together and add a dab of glue. Allow to dry and trim off the ends.

To make the ring

1 Turn the flower over. Take the 16 in- (40 cm-) nylon thread through 1 of the orange seed beads, placing the flower in the center of the thread.

2 String onto each end of the thread: 1 coral-red seed bead, 1 orange seed bead, and 1 coral-red seed bead. Add 1 orange seed bead to one end of the thread, and pull the opposite end through this last bead to cross the threads. You will now have a small loop.

3 Repeat step 2 until you have a chain of loops the size of your finger. Do not add the last orange seed bead to the final loop. Pass the 2 threads through 1 of the orange seed beads of the flower, in order to make the ring. Knot the threads together. Dab on some glue. Allow to dry and trim off.

VARIATIONS

You can make a more discreet flower by using smaller paillettes, or reduce or increase the number of paillettes used. Remember, the ring will be bulkier if you add more paillettes.

To make a bracelet, extend the chain that forms the ring shape and use larger beads, such as 4 mm-faceted ones.

This ring can also be adapted to make a sautoir (see page 104)— just add the flower to the end of a chain.

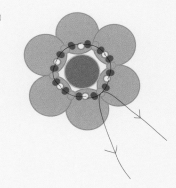

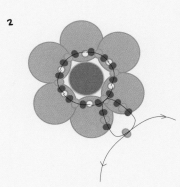

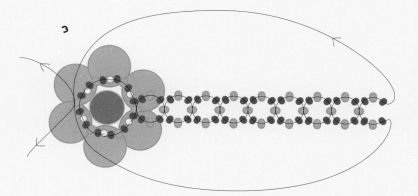

POMPOM

The bezel of this ring is like a ball of bright gems.
Have fun wearing two rings together, placing the bobbles side by side.

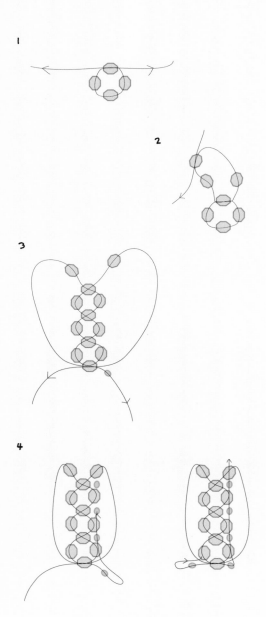

MATERIALS (for the white version)

For the bobble
- 24 in (60 cm) nylon thread (size 0)
- 12 white matte faceted Czech glass beads (4 mm)
- 8 white matte faceted Czech glass beads (3 mm)
- 8 red seed beads (11/0)
- scissors

For the ring
- 6 in (15 cm) nylon thread (size 0)
- approx. 18 white matte faceted Czech glass beads (3 mm)
- 8 red seed beads (11/0)
- scissors

To make the bobble

1 Cut the piece of nylon thread into 2 equal pieces. String 4 of the larger faceted beads (4 mm) onto 1 of the strands and pull them to the center. Fold the thread in half and pass one end through a bead to create a small loop.

2 Add 2 beads to one end of the thread and 1 bead to the other end. Pass the thread with the single bead through the middle bead to make a second loop.

3 Repeat step 2 once more. Finish by stringing a single bead onto each end of the thread. Pull each end of the thread through the first bead to make the round shape of the bobble. Add a seed bead to one end of the thread.

4 Take this same thread through each faceted bead, working around the bobble and adding a seed bead between every 2 faceted beads. Repeat this on the other side of the bobble with the other end of the thread. Knot the 2 threads together and add a dab of glue. Allow to dry and trim off the thread.

5 Thread 1 of the smaller faceted beads (3 mm) onto the other strand of thread. Double the thread and take the two ends through the center of the bobble to embed the faceted bead between 2 beads.

6 String 2 more faceted beads on this doubled thread: they will fit into the hollows of the bobble. Add 1 last faceted bead to one end of the thread, then draw the other end through the same bead to secure it. Pass one end of the thread through one of the three hollows in the bobble, string on 1 faceted bead, then repeat this step to conceal the other hollows. The bobble is finished. Make 2 tight knots and add a drop of glue. Allow to dry and trim off the thread.

To make the ring

7 Draw the 6 in- (15 cm-) piece of nylon thread through the lower part of the bobble, leaving an equal amount of thread on each side. Working on each thread in turn, string on 2 faceted beads and 1 seed bead alternately, until you have achieved the desired length. To finish, tie both ends together in a tight knot, add a drop of quick-drying glue, and when it has dried, trim off the thread.

VARIATIONS

The ring can also be made in a single color. Alternating the beads, as in this design, makes it slightly more difficult to work out the exact length required.

Once you have mastered the technique of weaving, you can use it to create other rings or other designs, such as a bracelet, for which all you need to do is alternate bobbles and beads on a length of nylon thread. To make the plain red design, replace the 4 mm-white faceted beads with 5 mm-red round beads, the 3 mm-white faceted beads with 4 mm-red faceted beads, and make the ring using seed beads.

5

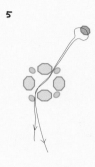

6

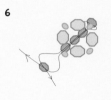

7

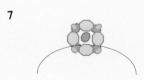

DIVA

The brilliance of this ring is due to the choice of a cabochon rhinestone—its oblong shape gives it a classic style that tempers the mix of colors and materials.

MATERIALS

- approx. 2 yds 15 in (2.2 m) nylon thread (size 0)
- 1 purple, oblong rhinestone, with 2 holes on each side (15 mm)
- approx. 30 silver faceted beads (3 mm)
- 20 lilac faceted beads (3 mm)
- 12 pink, round faux pearls (2 mm)
- scissors
- quick-drying glue

1 Cut a 1⅓ yd- (1.2 m-) strand of nylon thread, and thread it through the rhinestone, in one hole and out the other one on the same side. Center the rhinestone on the thread, and fold it in half to make 2 equal lengths. Thread 1 silver and 1 lilac bead on one end. Add 1 silver bead to the other end. Cross the threads through the lilac bead, back through the silver beads, and then through the rhinestone holes to the opposite side.

2 Balance the design by repeating this step on the other side. Take the nylon thread back to the starting point by passing it back through the silver beads and behind the rhinestone. Take the bottom thread and cross it through the top silver bead. Start to make a collar around the rhinestone by stringing 1 lilac bead onto one end of the thread and 1 silver bead onto the other. Cross the threads through the silver bead.

3 Continue alternating the silver and lilac beads in this fashion, forming a collar around the rhinestone. Using only one of the threads, string on the pearls one after another, inserting each between 2 faceted beads. Knot the 2 threads together. Add a drop of glue, allow to dry, and trim off.

4 To make the ring, thread 39 in (1 m) of nylon through 1 lilac faceted bead in the middle of the design you have just made, making sure you have an equal length on each side. String 1 silver bead onto each end. Add 1 lilac bead to one side only. Cross the threads through the lilac bead to make a loop. Make as many loops as necessary to fit your finger, then add 1 silver bead to each length of thread. Take the threads through 1 lilac bead on the opposite side of the design. Strengthen the closure by taking the thread through several beads. Add a drop of glue, allow to dry, and trim off closely.

VARIATION

You could also use a round rhinestone as the centerpiece of the ring, and glue it onto the template of a ring mount. The central stone and surrounding beads will sit well on the flat surface.

1

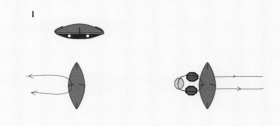

2

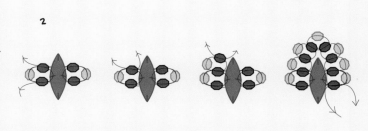

3

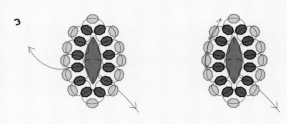

4

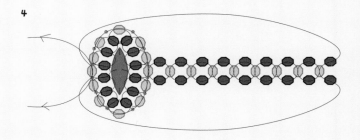

AS YOU LIKE IT, instructions page 64

62

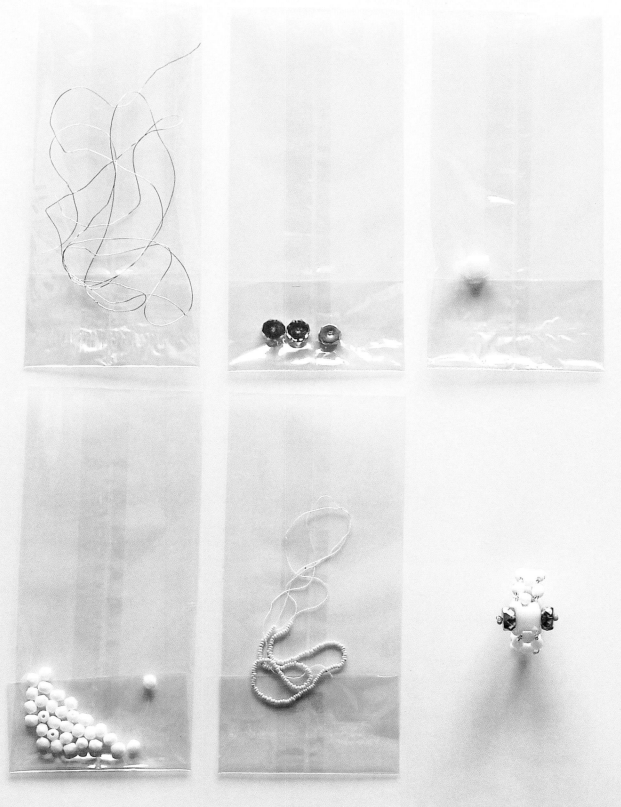

GADGET, instructions page 65

AS YOU LIKE IT

Circles of beads make a succession of loops that enable you to wear this ring whichever way you like it. Slip a single loop on your finger to display a sumptuous flower or wear several loops to show a minimalist petal.

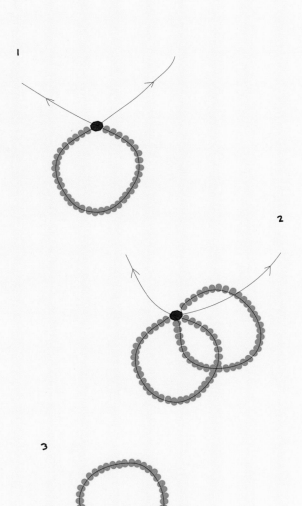

MATERIALS

• 39 in (1 m) nylon thread (size 0)
• approx. 400 red opaque seed beads (11/0)
• 3 black opaque faceted beads (3 mm)
• scissors
• quick-drying glue

1 String approximately 45 red seed beads onto the thread, then cross the ends through 1 faceted bead. You should have a loop 2³⁄₈ in (6 cm) in diameter. Adjust to the size of your finger by adding or removing beads as necessary.

2, 3 Repeat this procedure twice, making sure to create identical loops by using the same number of beads and passing the thread through the same faceted bead each time. Add a second faceted bead, then make 2 more loops, this time passing the thread through the second bead. Add the last faceted bead, then make 2 final loops. Knot the threads together. Add a drop of glue, allow to dry, then trim off the thread.

VARIATIONS

The size of this ring is up to you. Make as many petals as you like. You can also make them in 2 different colors.

We have used multiple loops as the basis for several ornaments, such as the necklaces "Aloha" (page 101) and "Snowdrop" (page 105)—this particular technique is a very creative starting point for jewelry design.

GADGET

The combination of a very simple hoop and a rather zany decoration makes a ring surprisingly playful and unique.

MATERIALS

For the hoop
- 18 in (45 cm) silver jewelry wire (28 gauge)
- approx. 30 white matte faceted Czech glass beads (4 mm)
- 2 white seed beads (11/0)

For the "gadget"
- 1 pale-pink opaque crystal cube (6 mm square)
- 2 silver faceted spacers (7 mm in diameter)
- 2 pale-pink seed beads (15/0)
- wire cutters

To make the hoop

1 String 4 faceted beads onto the wire and slide to the center. Double over the wire to obtain two ends. Take one end of the wire through the last bead.

2 Add 2 faceted beads to one side of the wire and a single bead to the other. Pass the side with the single bead through the top bead on the other side, making a loop. Repeat this step until you achieve a chain of the required length to fit your finger.

3 Finish by adding 1 white seed bead to each end of the chain. Pull each end of the wire through the first bead to make the hoop.

To make the "gadget"

4 Cross each end of the wire through the pink cube.

5 Add 1 spacer and 1 pink seed bead to the wire on one side of the cube. Repeat on the other side.

6 Pull the wires back through the cube several times, using the seed bead to secure the spacer. Trim off the wire with wire cutters.

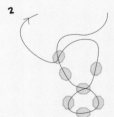

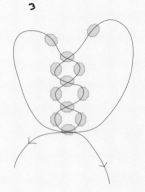

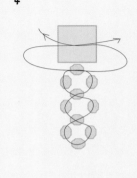

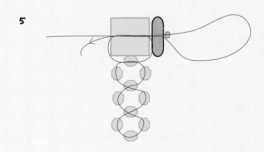

FREEWHEELER

This flexible, multiple-loop ring just twines around your fingers.
Arrange the loops around one finger or more for terrific variety and contrast.

MATERIALS

- 32 in (80 cm) nylon thread (size 0)
- approx. 200 coral-red seed beads (13/0)
- 1 brown, plain bead with a large hole
- 68 peach seed beads (11/0)
- 6 silver transparent bugle beads
- 2 faux pearls (3 mm)
- 2 small silver crimp beads
- flat-nose pliers
- scissors

1 String approximately 53 coral-red seed beads onto the nylon thread, then cross both ends of the thread through the brown bead. You should have a loop 2 3/8 in (6 cm) in diameter. Adjust the size to fit the width of your finger by adding or subtracting beads as necessary. Repeat this step twice, keeping the loops smooth and passing the threads through the plain bead each time. You should now have 3 loops and 2 lengths of nylon thread, A and B.

2 On thread A, string 13 peach seed beads and take the thread back through the first peach seed bead to make a loop. Then string on 5 more peach seed beads, 2 coral-red seed beads, 1 bugle bead, 3 coral-red seed beads, 1 bugle bead, 7 coral-red seed beads, and 1 faux pearl. Finish with a crimp bead. Crimp it with flat-nose pliers and trim off the thread.

3 On thread B, string 50 peach seed beads and pull the thread back through the first peach seed bead to make a loop. Add 15 coral-red seed beads to the same thread, then pull it through the bead at the bottom of the loop to make a smaller loop. String on 2 bugle beads, 1 coral-red seed bead, 1 bugle bead, 1 coral-red seed bead, 1 bugle bead, 3 coral-red seed beads, and 1 faux pearl. Finish with a crimp bead. Crimp, and trim off the thread.

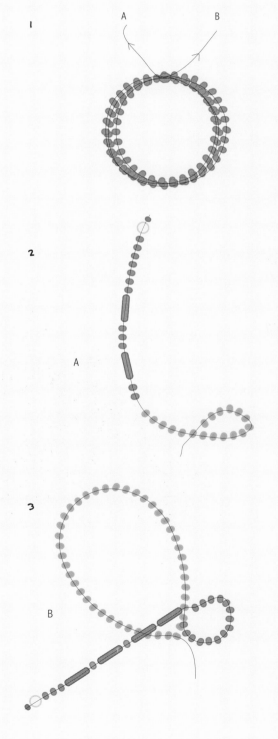

BLUE NOTE

When you wear this ring, the crystals turn on your finger and their facets catch the light at every angle.

MATERIALS (for the blue crystal version)

- 12 in (30 cm) nylon thread (size 0)
- approx. 24 blue crystal bicones (5 mm)
- approx. 20 black luster seed beads (11/0)
- scissors
- quick-drying glue

1 Alternating the beads, string 4 crystal beads and 4 seed beads onto the nylon thread.

2 Move the beads to the center of the thread and double it to obtain two equal lengths. Cross one end through the middle seed bead to make a circle.

3 On one end, string on 1 crystal, 1 seed bead, 1 crystal, and 1 seed bead. Thread 1 crystal, 1 seed bead, and 1 crystal onto the other end. Cross this thread through the last seed bead. Repeat this step until you have reached the desired length to fit your finger.

4 To finish, create a circle by bringing the two ends together. Add 1 crystal shape to each thread, pass the threads through several beads, and then knot them together. Add a dab of quick-drying glue, allow it to dry, and trim off.

1

2

3

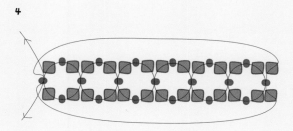

4

NECKLACES

CRYSTAL BALL, instructions page 76

BUTTON CHOKER, instructions page 77

SNOWFLAKES, instructions page 78

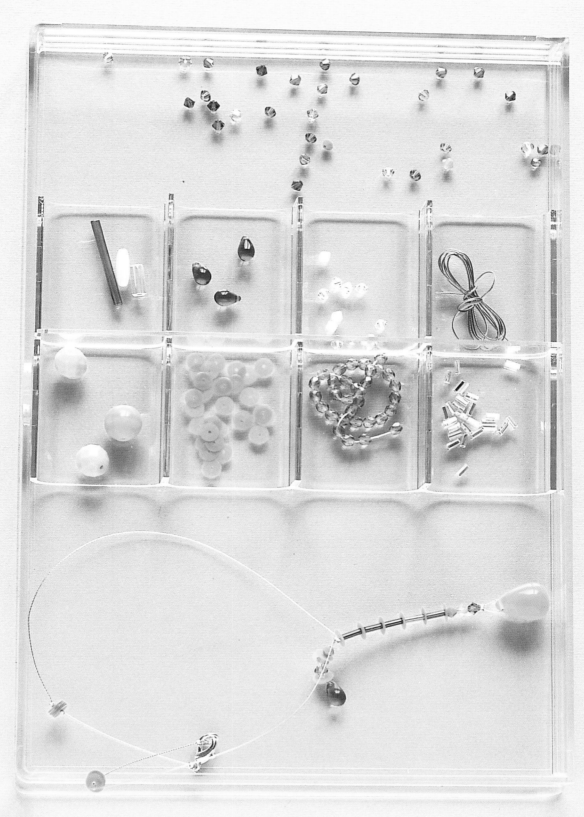

TEARDROP, instructions page 79

CRYSTAL BALL

This necklace uses few materials—its success relies upon a contrast of shapes and a play of light. The collar on top of the large bead sits like a sparkling crown. It is a pretty way to show off the marvelous sparkle of the crystal beads.

MATERIALS

- 1⅓ yds (1.2 m) embroidery ribbon (⅛ in/3 mm wide)
- 20 in (50 cm) black jewelry wire (28 gauge)
- 1 large, copper-colored, round hollow bead (20 mm)
- 4 copper clamshell knot covers (3 mm)
- 16 violet crystal bicones (3 mm)
- 8 pink translucent crystal bicones (3 mm)
- 1 smoke-brown beveled glass bead (7 mm)
- 1 large-eyed needle
- wire cutters
- scissors
- quick-drying glue

1 Cut the ribbon into 2 equal pieces. Using a large-eyed needle, thread the 2 ribbons through the large bead. Make several knots in the ends of the ribbon. Add 2 knot covers, put a drop of glue inside each one, then close them tightly. Use wire cutters to trim off the hook that sticks out of each knot cover, leaving only the round part.

2 Leaving 2 in (5 cm) of ribbon between the knot covers and the large bead, knot both ribbons to secure the bead.

3 Make the collar of beads. Center 1 violet crystal, 1 pink crystal, 1 violet crystal, and 1 pink crystal on the jewelry wire. Cross one end of the wire through the last violet crystal to make a circle.

4 Add 1 violet crystal and 1 pink crystal to one end of the wire, and 1 pink crystal to the other end. Cross the second wire through the violet crystal and repeat this operation 3 more times. Make a final loop by threading 1 pink crystal onto each end and crossing the wire through the first violet crystal. This closes the ring, making a collar. Take the wire back through a few more beads before trimming it off. Thread the ribbons at the top of the large bead through the collar, then through the beveled bead. Knot twice to secure all the beads. Add a knot cover to each end of the ribbon, as in step 1. To wear this necklace, simply tie the ribbons around your neck.

HINT

To close the necklace, you could also tie the ribbons in a double knot and pull it over your head.

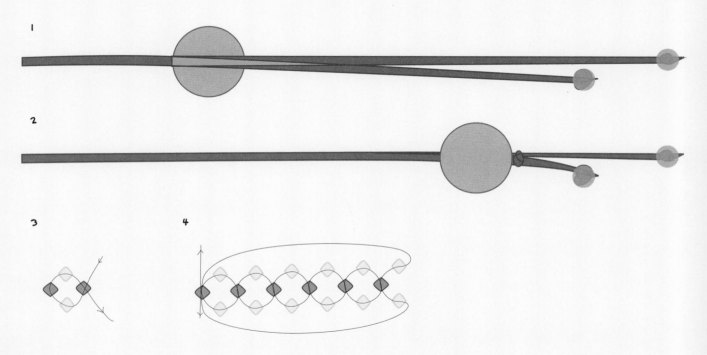

BUTTON CHOKER

The charm of this choker lies in its proportions: a very large button is boldly mounted on a pretty, delicate ribbon. Almost a caricature, in its size and the size of the holes, the button serves as a central ornament.

MATERIALS

- 32 in (80 cm) violet embroidery ribbon (1/8 in/3 mm wide)
- 1 large, violet 2-hole mother-of-pearl button (2 in/50 mm in diameter)
- 2 silver clamshell knot covers
- 1 silver spring-ring clasp
- 1 large-eyed needle
- scissors
- quick-drying glue

1 Cut the ribbon into two 16 in- (40 cm-) pieces. Take 1 piece of ribbon through one buttonhole and center the button. Use a large-eyed sewing needle to draw one end of the length of ribbon through the other length, securing the button in the center of the ribbon. Repeat this procedure with the other piece of ribbon in the other buttonhole.

2 Measure your neck to adjust the length of the ribbons (around 6 1/4 in/16 cm on each side of the button). Knot the two ends of the ribbon together on each side and add a knot cover to both. Add a drop of glue and close. Attach the clasp to the knot cover.

HINT

You can dress up this choker by pushing a fabric flower or a pretty feather through one of the buttonholes.

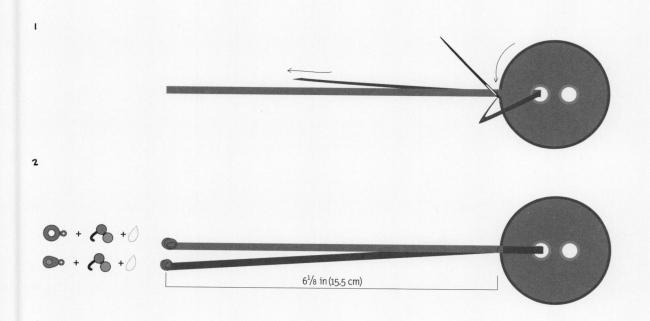

6 1/8 in (15.5 cm)

SNOWFLAKES

This necklace combines the subtlety of its two white crystal snowflakes with the blue nuances of the ribbon. You can wear it in several ways—as a delicate scarf, a discreet choker, or even a pretty belt.

MATERIALS

- 2 yds (1.8 m) nylon thread (size 0)
- approx. 64 white opaque faceted beads (4 mm)
- 6 copper eye pins (2 in/50 mm)
- 6 copper head pins (1½ in/38 mm)
- 6 white, round opaque glass beads (6 mm)
- 10 white crystal bicones (3 mm)
- 8 white crystal bicones (5 mm)
- 2 copper jump rings
- 2 copper clamshell knot covers
- 39 in (1 m) blue-gray embroidery ribbon (³/₁₆ in/4 mm wide)
- flat-nose pliers
- round-nose pliers
- wire cutters
- scissors
- quick-drying glue

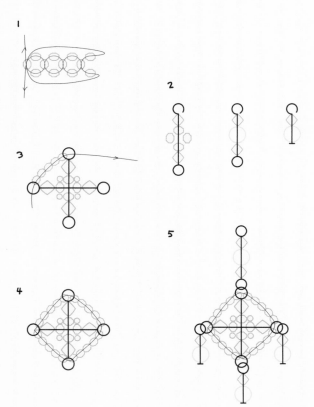

1 Cut the nylon thread into 6 equal lengths. String 4 white faceted beads (4 mm) onto 1 thread and slide them to the center. Fold the thread to obtain two equal sides. Take one end of the thread back through the last bead, making a loop. Add 2 more beads to one end and 1 bead to the other end. Cross this end through the second bead of the first thread to form another loop. Repeat this step once more, then add a bead to each end of thread. Pull both threads through to the very first bead to make a bobble. Knot the 2 threads together to secure it, then add a drop of quick-drying glue. Allow to dry, and trim off the thread.

2 Take 1 of the eye pins and thread on 1 crystal (5 mm), 1 previously made bobble, and 1 crystal (5 mm). Using wire cutters, trim the eye pin, leaving enough space to make a loop at the end. Use round-nose pliers to form the loop, but do not close it fully. On another eye pin, thread 1 crystal (3 mm), 1 round bead, and 1 crystal (3 mm). Trim and make a loop as before. On each of the 3 head pins, thread 1 round bead and 1 crystal (3 mm). To keep the beads in place on the pins, trim the head pin and make a loop at each end with round-nose pliers, but do not close them fully.

3 Thread 1 crystal (5 mm) onto another eye pin and fix it crosswise through the bobble of the first pin made. Add another crystal (5 mm). To keep the beads in place, trim the eye pin, and make a loop at the tip of the pin with round-nose pliers, but do not close it fully.

4 Take 1 of the lengths of thread through the head of 1 of the eye pins on the cross shape. String on 5 faceted beads, then continue adding sets of 5, turning around the cross and taking the thread through the head of each pin. Finish by knotting the two ends of the thread together. Add a dab of glue, allow to dry, then trim off.

5 Attach the little charms you have made to the arms of the cross, fixing the longer eye pin to the top, and the head pins to each arm and the foot. Close all the loops firmly with round-nose pliers. Make a second pendant in the same way. Attach a jump ring to the top of each pendant. Make a knot in each end of the ribbon, add a drop of glue, then slide each knot into a knot cover. Close firmly with the help of flat-nose pliers. Attach a pendant to each knot cover.

VARIATIONS

Make two extra bobbles and hang them from the bottom of each pendant (see photograph, page 74), or make a larger pendant by using bigger beads.

The color of the ribbon is just as important as the shape of the pendant. Play around with colors until you find a combination you like.

TEARDROP

You can make this delicate necklace in no time. The light, ethereal glass teardrop is enchanting.

MATERIALS

- 26 in (65 cm) soft-flex wire (20 in/50 cm for the necklace and 6 in/15 cm for the pendant)
- 1 large, turquoise-blue opaque glass drop
- 9 small, silver crimp beads
- 6 crystal bicones in mixed shades of blue and green
- 20 lime-green opaque sequins (6 mm)
- 5 bugle beads in mixed shades of blue and violet
- 1 small, turquoise transparent glass teardrop
- 1 silver lobster-claw clasp
- flat-nose pliers
- wire cutters

To make the lower part of the pendant

1 Thread the large glass drop onto the 6 in- (15 cm-) wire. Fold the wire, leaving only ¾ in (2 cm) of wire on one side. Thread a crimp bead on both wires and crimp it with flat-nose pliers. Using wire cutters, trim off the short end of wire close to the crimp, leaving only one end to work on.

2 Thread 3 crystal bicones onto the wire, then alternate between 6 sequins and 5 bugle beads, ending with a sequin. Add a crimp bead and pass the 20 in- (50 cm-) wire through it, making sure the crimp bead is in the middle of the wire. Crimp firmly.

To make the upper part of the pendant

3 Working with the end of the pendant wire, thread on 1 crystal, 1 sequin, 2 crystals, 1 sequin, and finish with the little turquoise drop. Add a crimp bead. Crimp it, then trim off the wire.

Necklace

4 Add 1 crimp bead to each end of the wire, 6 in (15 cm) from the top and crimp them. Add 6 sequins to each wire and secure them with a crimp bead. Fold over the ends of the wire and attach a crimp bead to each end, leaving a small loop. Attach each half of the clasp to a different loop and trim off the wire.

VARIATION

You could decorate the necklace wire even more by covering it with groups of sequins, securing them with crimp beads from time to time.

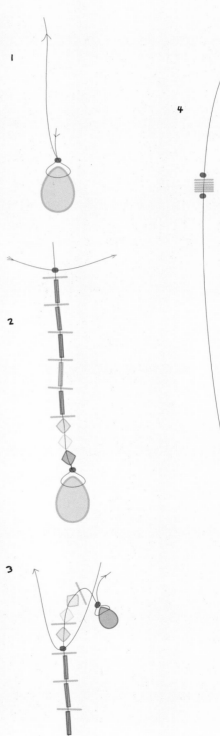

GREEN GODDESS, instructions page 84

ANOMALY, instructions page 85

BLOSSOM, instructions page 86

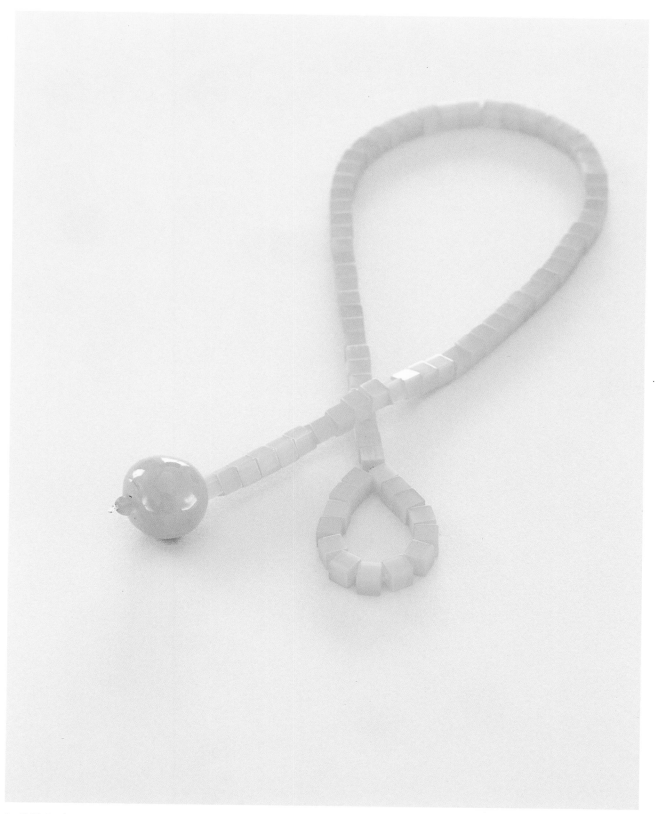

LITTLE YELLOW, instructions page 87

GREEN GODDESS

The airy, psychedelic choker sparkles like a fireworks display.
Its numerous, little antennae will shake and glitter around your neck.

1

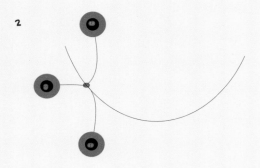

2

MATERIALS

- approx. 1½ yds (1.3 m) silver soft-flex wire
- approx. 55 small, silver crimp beads
- 22 black sequins (¼ in/5 mm)
- 22 green sequins (½ in/12 mm)
- 1 silver clasp
- flat-nose pliers
- wire cutters

1 Cut the wire into one length of 14 in (35 cm) (or the correct length to fit around your neck) and 22 lengths of 1½ in (4 cm). Make the little branches by placing 1 crimp bead on the tip of each short piece of wire, crimp it with flat-nose pliers, then add 1 black sequin and 1 large green sequin. Secure them with another crimp bead. Make 22 branches in total.

2 Add 1 crimp bead to the 14 in- (35 cm-) length of wire. Pull it to the middle of the wire, then insert the tips of 2–4 branches, adjusting the length of each branch as desired. Trim the ends of the wire branches and crimp the bead. Repeat this operation around the wire necklace, placing the branches symmetrically. Attach the clasp by threading 1 crimp bead on both ends and pull each wire through the loop in either half of the clasp. Bring the wire back through the crimp bead and crimp it. Trim off with wire cutters.

VARIATION

You could just use seed beads to decorate the necklace wire for a more subdued effect.

ANOMALY

Large lampwork glass beads in a daring mix of tropical colors stand out boldly on this necklace. Fish, clowns, or anemones, choose whatever metaphor for these beads that takes your fancy.

MATERIALS

- 2¹⁄₂ yds (2.2 m) nylon thread (size 0)
- 2 orange sequins (³⁄₈ in/10 mm)
- 3 orange, round glass beads (8 mm)
- 2 lampwork glass beads (30 mm) (see page 6)
- approx. 100 orange matte transparent seed beads (9/0)
- approx. 80 orange matte opaque seed beads (11/0)
- approx. 30 white faceted beads (3 mm)
- approx. 360 green opaque seed beads (9/0)
- scissors
- quick-drying glue

1 Make a knot in one end of the thread. Apply some quick-drying glue and allow to dry. String on 1 sequin, 1 round glass bead, 9 orange matte transparent seed beads, 1 large lampwork bead, 1 round glass bead, 24 orange matte transparent seed beads, and 1 white faceted bead.

2 Next, thread on 36 in (90 cm) of beads, alternating between the two types of seed beads and faceted beads and gradually incorporating the green seed beads. When you reach within 4 in (10 cm) from the end, take the thread back through the white faceted bead on the other end.

3 Finish by adding 2³⁄₄ in (7 cm) of orange matte transparent seed beads, the large lampwork bead, 6 orange matte transparent seed beads, 1 round glass bead, and 1 sequin. Tie a knot in the thread, apply quick-drying glue, and trim off.

HINT

The secret of this necklace's success lies in choosing glass lampwork beads: their weight will help it to sit beautifully.

BLOSSOM

A huge flower made from yellow beads brings this very classic sautoir up to date.
You can make it as long as you like: It can even be worn like a bandolier, slung across
one shoulder.

1

2

3

MATERIALS

- 1³/₄ yds (1.6 m) nylon thread (size D)
- 1 spool of silver jewelry wire (28 gauge)
- approx. 150 faux pearls (8 mm)
- approx. 2500 yellow seed beads (11/0)
- 1 yellow, round plastic button with a hook (approx. 1 in/25 mm in diameter)
- wire cutters
- scissors
- quick-drying glue

1 String all the freshwater pearls onto the nylon thread. Tie the ends together with several knots. Add a dab of glue, allow to dry, and trim off the threads.

2 Cut a 6 in- (15 cm-) length of jewelry wire with wire cutters and thread on the seed beads. Fold the wire in half and pass one end through the first seed bead, making a loop. Take another 6 in- (15 cm-) length of wire, thread the end of the wire through the first loop, and string on more seed beads. When it is about a quarter full, anchor the wire through a bead from the first loop. Add more beads, then attach the wire to the first loop again, and continue adding beads and attaching the wire to the first loop twice more. Finish by taking the end of the wire back through the first seed bead. Twist the wires together. Repeat this step, making as many loops/petals as you wish.

3 Arrange the petals in a flower shape. Fix the large button in the center of the flower with nylon thread. Make several knots. Add a dab of glue, allow to dry, and trim the threads. Attach the flower similarly to the necklace with nylon thread.

VARIATION

You could also simply attach a fabric flower to the pearl necklace.

+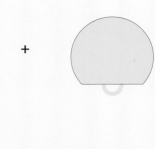

LITTLE YELLOW

Weight and counterweight ... this necklace flows around the neck. It's simple and solid, the flamboyant color making its only statement. The closing loop is very easy to make and contributes to the simple style.

MATERIALS

- 32 in (80 cm) nylon thread (size B)
- 2 small silver crimp beads
- 1 yellow, round matte transparent bead (5 mm)
- 1 yellow, round ceramic bead (20 mm)
- approx. 82 yellow, pearly opaque cube beads (6 mm)
- flat-nose pliers
- scissors

I Make a knot at one end of the nylon thread, add a crimp bead, and crimp with flat-nose pliers. Thread on the small bead, the large bead, 72 cube beads, 1 crimp bead, and 10 more cube beads. Pull the thread back through the crimp bead. Make sure that the large bead will fit through this loop—adjust if necessary by adding more cube beads. Secure the loop with the crimp bead. Trim off the thread. You now have a loop through which the bead will pass to close the necklace.

HINT

You can adapt the length of the necklace to make a choker or a long chain.

TRAVELER'S TALE

The beads that hang so prettily from this necklace could be charming images in the pages of a travel diary. They make a pretty "lantern", like a souvenir from some faraway place.

1

2

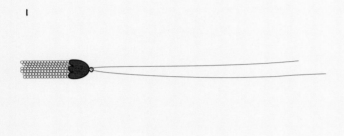

3

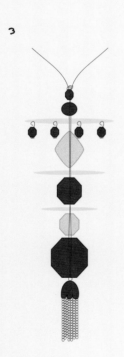

MATERIALS

- 32 in (80 cm) thick, black cotton thread
- 1 copper tassel pendant
- approx. 10 black faceted beads (3 mm)
- approx 9 small, copper head pins
- 3 decorative mother-of-pearl buttons, perforated with holes (preferably in 3 graduated sizes approx. 1 in/25 mm, 3/4 in/20 mm, 5/8 in/15 mm in diameter)
- 1 large, black faceted bead (15 mm)
- 1 copper faceted bead (8 mm)
- 1 medium, black faceted bead (10 mm)
- 1 copper, bicone faceted bead (15 mm)
- 1 black, round bead (5 mm)
- 2 black faceted beads (6 mm)
- 2 black crystal bicones (3 mm)
- 1 black glass paillette (15 mm)
- 2 large, copper crimp beads
- 1 black glass drop
- flat-nose pliers
- round-nose pliers
- wire cutters
- scissors

1 Center the tassel on the thread.

2 Prepare the charms. Place 1 black 3 mm-faceted bead on each head pin. Trim the pins to 1/2 in (10 mm) with wire cutters. Using round-nose pliers, make a loop. Hang the charms from the holes of the largest button and close the loops firmly (you may need to adjust the number of charms according to the number of holes in your button).

3 Bring together the 2 lengths of thread. String on the large, black faceted bead, the copper faceted bead, the smallest button, the medium, black faceted bead, the medium-sized button, the copper, bicone faceted bead, the large button decorated with charms, and the black, round bead. Finish with a 3 mm-black faceted bead. Make a double knot to secure the beads. Leave about 2 3/8 in (6 cm), then knot each thread separately. Add a 6 mm-faceted bead to each thread, then knot again. Measure 3 1/8 in (8 cm) and make a knot in each thread. Add 1 crystal bicone to each side and knot again. Knot the 2 threads together several times, leaving about 1 1/2 in (4 cm) thread on each end. String the paillette on one end, add a crimp bead, and crimp with flat-nose pliers. Trim the thread. Add the black glass drop to the end of the other thread, followed by a crimp bead. Crimp and trim the thread.

HINT

You could decorate each of the buttons with charms, not just the largest one.

VELVET REVOLUTION

This very discreet little choker is made from small flat buttons sewn onto soft velvet ribbon—the alternating circles and squares are enlivened by little "whiskers" that pop up every now and again.

MATERIALS

- 20 in (50 cm) burgundy velvet ribbon ($\frac{1}{4}$ in/7 mm wide)
- 2 decorative, copper clamshell knot covers ($\frac{3}{8}$ in/10 mm in diameter)
- red and black Polyester sewing thread
- 8 white, square mother-of-pearl buttons ($\frac{1}{4}$ in/7 mm in diameter)
- 7 white, round mother-of-pearl buttons ($\frac{1}{4}$ in/7 mm in diameter)
- 8$\frac{3}{4}$ in (21 cm) nylon thread (size 0)
- 7 black seed beads (15/0)
- 7 red seed beads (15/0)
- flat-nose pliers
- sewing needle
- scissors
- quick-drying glue
- superglue

1 Make a knot at each end of the ribbon. Add a drop of glue. Place each knot in a knot cover and close them, using flat-nose pliers.

2 Leave 3$\frac{1}{4}$ in (8 cm) of ribbon, then sew on 1 square button, using the red and black Polyester thread together. The stitches should be visible. Leave about $\frac{1}{2}$ in (15 mm), then sew on 1 round button. Work like this, alternating the buttons, until you have used them all, spacing them evenly around the choker.

3 Now make the "whiskers". Cut the nylon thread into 7 lengths of 1$\frac{1}{4}$ in (3 cm). Using a needle, thread a length of nylon thread through both holes of each round button so that you have 2 short threads sticking up from the button holes. Dab a drop of superglue on each tip, then add 1 black seed bead to one tip and 1 red one to the other. Allow to dry.

HINT

This choker just ties around the neck and is worn like a dog-collar. To make it more formal, leave out the little nylon "whiskers".

I

2

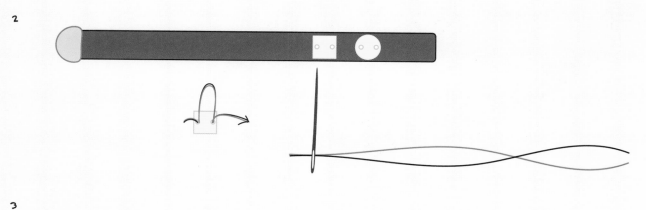

3

BUTTON QUEEN

Who has not at some time been fascinated by the contents of an old sewing-box filled with bobbins and a myriad of multicolored buttons? They have so many stories to tell and need only to be strung and shown to add a cheerful touch to an outfit.

MATERIALS
- $4^1/_3$ yds (4 m) strong, red Polyester thread
- 54 plastic buttons, assorted colors ($^3/_8$–$^3/_4$ in/10–20 mm in diameter)
- scissors

I Cut the thread in half. Knot the 2 pieces together at one end. Lay the buttons out on a board and plan the order of arrangement, working to balance the rhythm of colors and shapes.

2 Pull 1 of the threads through a button from underneath. Take it back through the opposite hole. Working with the other thread, proceed in the opposite fashion, pulling it through the top of the button, then back through the opposite buttonhole. Knot the 2 threads to secure the button. Secure all the buttons in this way. To close the necklace, knot the threads tightly together.

VARIATION
Make the necklace with identical buttons for a very chic effect.

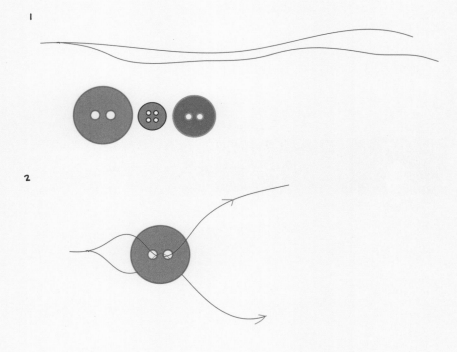

COURTISAN, instructions page 96

PENDULUM, instructions page 97

COURTISAN

What can be more intriguing and sensual than red lace? Here, it makes a simple and original support for a pendant made from mother-of-pearl buttons.

MATERIALS

- approx. 13 in (33 cm) red lace ($^5/_8$ in/15 mm wide)
- 2 flat, silver ribbon crimp-ends (15 mm)
- 2 silver jump rings
- 1 silver screw clasp
- 20 in (50 cm) red embroidery ribbon ($^3/_{16}$ in/4 mm wide)
- 3 silver clamshell knot covers
- 4 red pearl buttons ($^5/_8$ in/15 mm in diameter)
- 4 green pearl buttons ($^5/_8$ in/15 mm in diameter)
- red Polyester sewing thread
- large-eyed needle
- 2 flat-nose pliers
- wire cutters
- scissors
- quick-drying glue

I Measure the lace around your neck to determine the correct length. Turn down a small hem at each end and attach the ribbon crimp-ends. Add jump rings, then attach each end of the clasp. To open a jump ring, use 2 flat-nose pliers. Twist the ring gently to open without distorting it, pulling one side of the ring towards you and the other side in the opposite direction. To close the ring, follow the same technique, using the 2 pliers.

2 Cut the embroidery ribbon in 2 equal lengths. Tie the 2 pieces together by knotting them $5^1/_2$ in (14 cm) from the end. Put a knot cover on the knot, add a dab of glue, and close the knot cover. Using wire cutters, trim off the loop. String 8 buttons on the shorter ends of ribbon, alternating the colors and working each ribbon through the holes as shown in the diagram. To finish the pendant, make a knot at each end of ribbon and place them in knot covers. Add a drop of glue, close, and trim off the loops using wire cutters.

3 Place the button pendant in the center of the lace. Attach it to the lace by weaving it through the gaps in the lace, using a large-eyed needle. Secure the ends of the ribbon to the back of the lace using red Polyester thread.

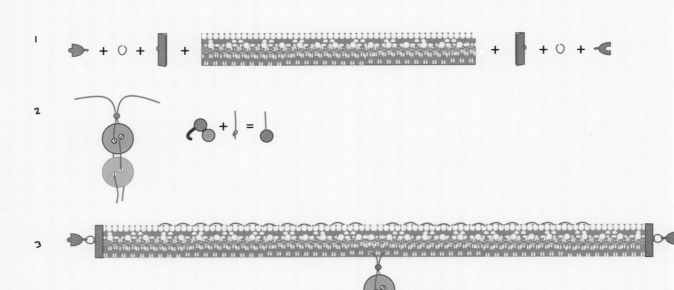

PENDULUM

The rounded forms of this pendant work well as a contrast to the rigid shape of the mount. This elegant choker can be endlessly varied, depending on the ornaments you have chosen to hang from it.

MATERIALS

- approx. 12 in (30 cm) silver soft-flex wire
- 7 small, silver crimp beads
- approx. 30 white seed beads (11/0)
- 1 large, white opaque glass drop (25 mm)
- 4 white sequins ($^5/_{16}$ in/8 mm in diameter)
- 1 white, round faceted bead (8 mm)
- 3 white opaque crystal bicones (3 mm)
- 1 white translucent crystal bicone (5 mm)
- 2 white faceted beads (4 mm)
- 2 white bugle beads (5 mm)
- 1 small, white opaque glass drop (10 mm)
- 2 white, flat, round glass beads (5 mm)
- 1 silver-plated neck hoop
- flat-nose pliers
- wire cutters

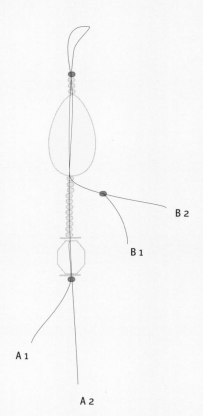

1 Cut a 6$^3/_4$ in- (17 cm-) length of soft-flex wire with wire cutters. Bend into a U-shape, with one end 4$^1/_4$ in (10.5 cm) long (wire A), and the other 2$^1/_2$ in (6.5 cm) long (wire B). Near the bend of the wire, add 1 crimp bead and crimp it with flat-nose pliers, leaving a loop around $^3/_{16}$ in (5 mm) in diameter.

2 With both wires A and B together, thread on 3 seed beads and the large glass drop. Separate the wires and, working on wire A only, thread on 11 seed beads, 1 sequin, the large round faceted bead, 1 sequin, and 1 crimp bead. Pass a 2 in- (5 cm-) length of wire through the faceted bead and the crimp bead and crimp with flat-nose pliers. You now have 2 branches: A1 and A2.

3 To branch A1, add 1 white opaque crystal, 1 seed bead, 1 white opaque crystal, 5 seed beads, 1 white opaque crystal, the white translucent crystal, then 1 seed bead. Finish with a crimp bead, and crimp it. Trim off the wire. On branch A2, add 1 faceted bead (4 mm), 1 bugle bead, 1 sequin, 1 seed bead, 1 crimp bead, and the small, white drop. Take the wire back through the crimp bead before closing it. Trim off the wire.

4 On wire B, string 6 seed beads, 1 round flat bead, and 1 crimp bead. Thread a 1$^1/_4$ in- (3 cm-) length of wire through the flat bead and the crimp bead and crimp. You now have 2 branches: B1 and B2.

5 On B1, add 1 round flat bead, 1 white bugle bead, and 2 seed beads. Finish with a crimp bead and crimp. Trim off the wire. On B2, add 3 seed beads, 1 faceted bead (4 mm), and 1 sequin. Finish with a crimp bead and crimp. Trim off the wire. Thread the pendant onto the silver hoop.

SPRING GARLAND

There's all the freshness of spring in this little necklace, decorated with colored glass leaves and berries. It's romantic and delicate—perfect for a spring wedding.

MATERIALS
• 1 silver-plated neck hoop

glass beads, with wire stems attached:
• 2 white flowers
• 6 yellow leaves
• 4 white drops
• 1 yellow drop
• 6 red drops

I Compose a mini still-life arrangement by carefully placing the beads on the hoop, attaching them by twisting the stems around the neck hoop as shown.

VARIATION
A choker made entirely from glass teardrops would also have a very pretty effect.

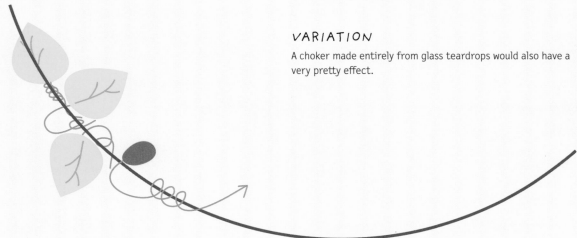

ALOHA

Like a welcoming garland of fresh flowers, this chain adds a touch of poetry and softness to a plain sweater.

MATERIALS

- 3¹/₃ yds (2.8 m) nylon thread (size 0)
- approx. 800 yellow opaque seed beads (11/0)
- approx. 1500 fluorescent-orange-lined crystal seed beads (11/0)
- scissors
- quick-drying glue

1 String yellow beads on the nylon thread for 8 in (20 cm). Add orange beads for 2¹/₂ in (6 cm).

2 Take the thread back through the first orange bead to make a loop.

3 Add another 2¹/₂ in (6 cm) of orange beads and take the thread back through the first orange bead. Repeat this operation 4 more times, making sure that all 6 orange "petals" are the same size. Repeat these steps until you have made 5 lengths of yellow beads and 5 orange flowers. Close the necklace by knotting the threads together. Add a drop of glue. Allow to dry, then trim off the ends.

VARIATION

Following the same method, make a chain of black seed beads with red flowers. The flowers will stand out against the black background with a striking effect!

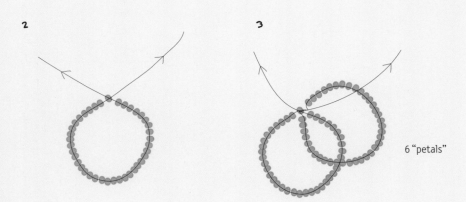

1

8 in (20 cm)　　　　2¹/₂ in (6 cm)

2

3

6 "petals"

ABACUS, instructions page 106

PUNCTUATION, instructions page 107

ALL THAT
JAZZ,

instructions
page 108

SNOWDROP, instructions page 109

ABACUS

Like a talisman or lucky charm, this necklace will bring happiness to its wearer.
Its graphic lines are the perfect foil for the sparkle of the silvery beads.

1½ in (4 cm)

MATERIALS

- 1¾ yds (1.62 m) silver soft-flex wire
- 22 small, silver crimp beads
- approx. 820 metallic-silver seed beads (11/0)
- approx. 24 black seed beads (9/0)
- approx. 30 blue-black seed beads (11/0)
- approx. 60 metallic pewter seed beads (11/0)
- 2 black crystal cubes (4 mm)
- flat-nose pliers
- wire cutters

1 Cut ten 3 in- (8 cm-) lengths of soft-flex wire with wire cutters. Add 1 crimp bead to the remaining length and crimp. Thread on 1 black cube, then enough silver seed beads to cover 32 in (80 cm). Add the second black cube and 1 crimp bead. Crimp it with flat-nose pliers and trim off the wire.

2 Gently bend the bead-decorated wire in half. Thread a 3 in- (8 cm-) length of wire between the last 2 silver beads at one end of the long wire, just above the crystal cube. Loop it round the wire, add a crimp bead to the end, and crimp it. Trim off the little bit of wire that sticks out.

3 String 1½ in (4 cm) of silver seed beads onto the horizontal wire. Thread the wire between the last 2 silver beads on the opposite end of the long wire, loop it around the wire, and add a crimp bead. Crimp and trim off. Continue working like this, making 10 rows of beads, alternating the sizes and colors: 10 rows of seed beads (6 silver, 1 black, 1 blue-black, 2 pewter).

VARIATION

You can vary the number of rows, adding more or less according to your design, or add a row or two of bugle beads or tiny pearls.

PUNCTUATION

The plain links of this chain are punctuated with delicate beads, their pearly luster contrasting with the copper finish of the chain. This is an arrangement that can be varied in many ways.

MATERIALS

- 28 in (70 cm) copper chain
- 1 copper lobster-claw clasp
- 2 copper jump rings
- 8 in (20 cm) jewelry wire (28 gauge)
- 10 gold-tone crimp beads
- 2 large, pink freshwater pearls (9 mm)
- 1 large, pale-green freshwater pearl (9 mm)
- 7 small, pink freshwater pearls (4 mm)
- 2 flat-nose pliers
- round-nose pliers
- wire cutters

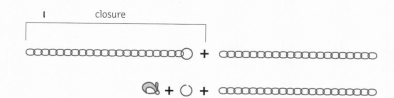

2

I Cut 3 lengths of chain with wire cutters: one 18 in (46 cm) long, one 5 in (13 cm) long, and another 4 in (10 cm) long. Attach a jump ring to each end of the longest piece of chain. Add the clasp to the jump ring on one end of the chain and attach the shortest chain to the jump ring at the other end. Attach the 5 in- (13 cm-) length to the center of the long chain. Use 2 flat-nose pliers to open the links of the chain and assemble the different pieces. Handle the jump rings gently, being careful not to pull them out of shape. Draw one side towards you and the other side away from you. To close the ring, proceed in the same fashion, using the 2 pliers.

2 Cut three ³/₄ in- (20 mm-) lengths and seven ¹/₂ in- (15 mm-) lengths of jewelry wire with wire cutters. Add a crimp bead to one end of each length and crimp it with flat-nose pliers, then add a freshwater pearl.

3 Make a loop in each pendant with round-nose pliers. Attach 1 small pearl pendant to the end of the shortest chain. Attach the other pendants at intervals to the links of the central chain, with the green pearl at the top and a cluster of pearls at the end of the chain, making sure to twist each loop several times through a link.

ALL THAT JAZZ

This long sautoir can be worn in different ways, even as a narrow belt. Contrasting colors and materials are used to enhance the beauty of the large molded plastic beads.

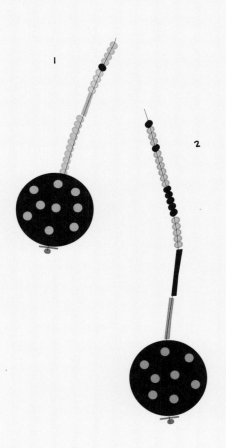

MATERIALS

- 1²/₃ yds (1.5 m) nylon thread (size 0)
- 2 small, silver crimp beads
- 2 pink sequins (³/₁₆ in/4 mm)
- 1 black, round plastic bead with orange spots (25 mm)
- 1 black, round plastic bead with pink spots (25 mm)
- 21 in (53 cm) black plastic lacing (see page 9)
- 7 in (17 cm) pink plastic lacing
- 12¹/₂ in (32 cm) orange plastic lacing
- approx. 60 orange matte transparent seed beads (8/0)
- approx. 120 pink transparent seed beads (11/0)
- approx. 60 orange opaque seed beads (11/0)
- flat-nose pliers
- scissors

1 Add a crimp bead to one end of the nylon thread. Crimp with flat-nose pliers, then add 1 sequin and the large black and pink bead. Next decorate the chain by alternating between different lengths of plastic lacing and seed beads. To achieve color harmony, start with pink lacing and pink seed beads close to the large pink bead, interspersing black lacing and beads, and then gradually introducing orange elements.

2 When you reach the end of the nylon thread, add the large black and orange bead, 1 sequin, and 1 crimp bead. Crimp with flat-nose pliers and trim off the thread.

HINT

You could also add in paillettes or even use lampwork beads (see "Glass Beads," page 6). Letting your imagination run riot is the key to success with this necklace.

SNOWDROP

Coiled around your neck, this romantic necklace creates a striking effect with the contrast between the colors and the textures of the seed beads.

MATERIALS

- 39 in (1 m) nylon thread (size 0)
- 1 silver spring clasp
- 2 silver crimp beads
- approx. 240 metallic pewter seed beads (10/0)
- approx 210 white opaque seed beads (10/0)
- 5 silver jump rings
- 2 flat-nose pliers
- scissors

1 Pass the nylon thread through the loop of the spring clasp. Thread on 1 crimp bead, then bring the thread back through the crimp bead. Crimp with flat-nose pliers and trim off the short end of the thread. Thread pewter seed beads on the long thread until you have covered 6½ in (16 cm).

2 Add 44 white seed beads, then take the thread back through the first white bead to make a loop. Repeat this operation 5 times, smoothing out the line of beads in the flower as you go. Then string on pewter beads for another 6½ in (16 cm).

3 Make a little chain with the 5 silver jump rings. Using 2 flat-nose pliers to open the rings, twist each ring gently, being careful not to pull it out of shape. Draw one side of the ring towards you and the other side in the opposite direction. To close each ring, proceed in the same manner, using the 2 pliers. Add 1 crimp bead to the end of the necklace. Take the thread back through one of the jump rings, then back through the crimp bead. Crimp and trim off.

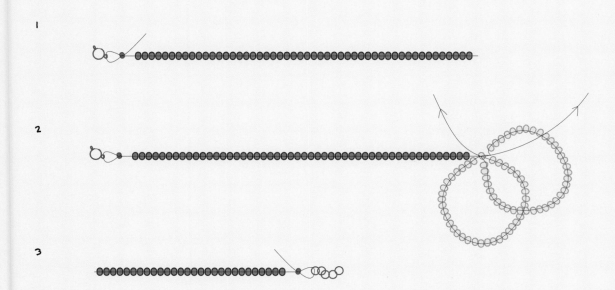

1

2

3

CONSTELLATION

In this unexpected combination of chains and ribbons, the large faux pearls look like a constellation of planets. Vary the links and the size of the pearls and simply complete the whole assembly with clamshell knot covers.

MATERIALS

- 2 in (5 cm) deep-pink embroidery ribbon ($3/16$ in/4 mm wide)
- $8\frac{1}{2}$ in (22 cm) deep-burgundy embroidery ribbon ($3/16$ in/ 4 mm wide)
- 8 in (20 cm) dark-plum embroidery ribbon ($3/16$ in/4 mm wide)
- $3\frac{1}{2}$ in (9 cm) thick, black cotton thread
- 10 copper clamshell knot covers
- 10 faux pearls (from $3/8$–1 in/8–25 mm in diameter)
- 10 copper eye pins
- $2\frac{3}{4}$ in (7 cm) copper chain with large links
- $2\frac{3}{4}$ in (7 cm) copper chain with medium links
- $3\frac{1}{4}$ in (8 cm) copper chain with small links
- flat-nose pliers
- round-nose pliers
- wire cutters
- quick-drying glue

1 Make a knot at each end of the ribbons and the thread. Put a crimp cover on each knot. Add a dab of glue and close the crimp cover with flat-nose pliers.

2 Attach an eye pin to each pearl. Trim off the stem of the pin with wire cutters, leaving approximately $\frac{1}{4}$ in (7 mm). Using round-nose pliers, make a loop, but do not close completely.

3 Make the chain by alternating the various elements: pearls, ribbons, thread, and chains.

HINT

Simplify the necklace by using chain alone. You will not need to attach any crimp covers, since the eye pins can be directly connected to the links of the chain.

1

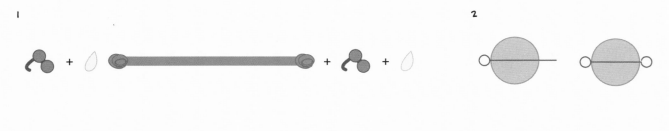

3

BROOCHES, PINS,

AND BRACELETS

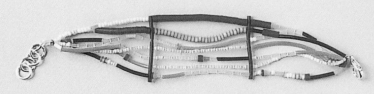

HEART OF GLASS, instructions page 116

LADYBUG, instructions page 117

HEART OF GLASS

The beads of this luscious, round brooch form successive circles. The contrast of matte and shiny beads gives it both a modern and retro feel—a jewel to cheer up a plain turtleneck sweater.

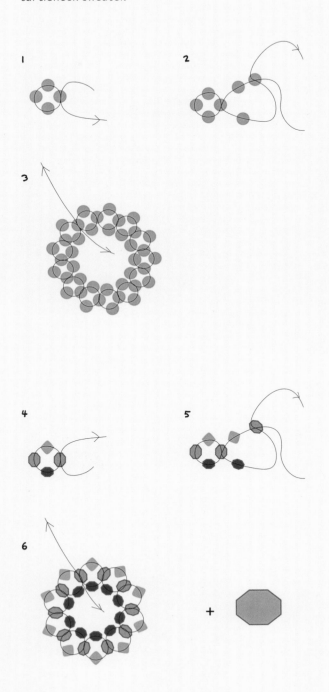

MATERIALS

- 2 yds 21 in (2.35 m) silver jewelry wire (28 gauge)
- 39 orange, round glass beads (5 mm)
- 1 gold-plated, round brooch mount with perforated template (1 3/8 in/35 mm in diameter)
- 10 burgundy transparent faceted beads (3 mm)
- 10 deep-pink transparent faceted beads (4 mm)
- 10 orange crystal bicones (3 mm)
- 1 burgundy transparent faceted bead (8 mm)
- flat-nose pliers
- wire cutters

1 Cut 5 pieces of wire in the following lengths: 39 in (1 m), 32 in (80 cm), 10 in (25 cm), 8 in (20 cm), and 4 in (10 cm). Working with the longest piece of wire, make the first collar (A). Thread 4 round beads and place them in the center of the wire. Fold in half and pull one end of the wire back through the first bead to produce a loop.

2 Add 1 bead to one end of the wire and 2 beads to the other end, bringing the wire back through the last bead. Repeat this step 10 more times. When you have made the last loop, add 1 orange bead to each end of the wire, then cross them through the very first bead to make a collar. Fasten it by pulling the wires through the beads several times and trimming the ends with wire cutters.

3 Using the 10 in- (25 cm-) wire, attach collar A to the perforated brooch template, working the wire through all the holes. Twist the wires together under the template. Trim off.

4 Working with the 32 in- (80 cm-) wire, make a second collar (B). Thread on 1 burgundy faceted bead, 1 pink faceted bead, 1 orange crystal, and 1 pink faceted bead. Center them on the wire, then pass one end of the wire through the last pink bead to make a loop.

5 Add 1 orange crystal and 1 pink faceted bead to one end of the wire and 1 burgundy faceted bead to the other end, bringing the wire back through the pink faceted bead. Repeat this step 7 more times. When you have made the last loop, add 1 orange crystal to one end and 1 burgundy faceted bead to the other. Cross the wires through the first pink faceted bead to make a collar (B). Fasten it by pulling the wires through the beads several times. Trim the wires.

6 Using the 8 in- (20 cm-) wire, attach collar B to the template, in the center of collar A. Twist the wires together under the template and trim off. Add the large burgundy bead in the center by threading on the 4 in- (10 cm-) wire and taking each end through a hole in the template. Twist the wires under the template and trim off. Fix the template to the brooch back. Close the claws, using flat-nose pliers.

LADYBUG

This little whimsical scenario takes no time at all to make and can be varied *ad infinitum*. You could use buttons and all sorts of charms: butterflies, dragonflies…

MATERIALS

- 39 in (1 m) black jewelry wire (28 gauge)
- 71 black seed beads (11/0)
- 83 red seed beads (11/0) (80 for the ladybug)
- 1 kilt pin
- 8 in (20 cm) black jewelry wire (30 gauge)
- 1 orange sequin ($^3/_{16}$ in/4 mm)
- 1 red faceted bead (8 mm)
- approx. 8 in (20 cm) red embroidery ribbon ($^1/_8$ in/3 mm wide)
- 1 black-and-white round bead (15 mm)
- 3 large silver crimp beads
- 1 small, silver crimp bead
- 1 fancy, black opaque faceted bead (8 mm)
- flat-nose pliers
- wire cutters
- scissors

1 To make the ladybug, follow the diagram, working with the 32 in- (80 cm-) black jewelry wire and the red and black seed beads, beginning at the bottom. Before you close the loop at the top, hang it over the lower part of the kilt pin. Finish the wires by pulling them back through several beads. Trim off the wire with wire cutters.

2 Double the remaining 8 in- (20 cm-) wire over the lower part of the kilt pin, make a loop, and twist the rest of the wire together to make a 1¼ in- (3 cm-) long stem. Add the sequin, 2 red seed beads, the faceted red bead, 1 red seed bead, and the small crimp bead. Using flat-nose pliers, crimp the crimp bead. Trim off the wire.

3 Cut the ribbon in half, thread one piece through the black-and-white bead. Center the bead and tie a knot just above it. Hang the ribbon over the kilt pin, then attach a large crimp bead close to the end. Crimp and trim the ribbon.

4 Attach a large crimp bead to the remaining piece of ribbon and crimp. Thread on the black opaque bead and 1 large crimp bead. Attach to the kilt pin by making a loop and passing the ribbon through the second crimp bead. Crimp and trim the ribbon.

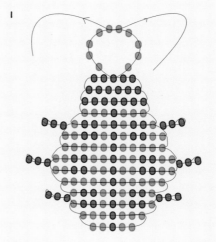

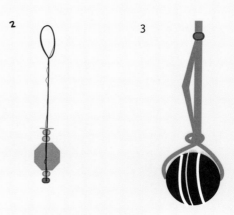

ILLUSIONS

To protect the delicate branches on this brooch from being crushed, wear it on a coat or a purse. Its trembling fragility and the chic combination of gilded metal, lime-green wire, and scintillating beads make it a most attractive pin that you almost hesitate to touch.

MATERIALS

• 2¼ yds (2 m) lime-green soft-flex wire
• approx. 90 small, gold-tone crimp beads
• 7 pink luster crystal bicones (5 mm)
• 12 pink luster crystal bicones (3 mm)
• 8 orange bugle beads (7 mm)
• approx. 300 lime-green, silver-lined seed beads (11/0)
• approx. 50 peach seed beads (11/0)
• approx. 50 pink-lined crystal seed beads (11/0)
• approx. 50 coral-pink transparent seed beads (11/0)
• approx. 14 pink opaque bugle beads (7 mm)
• approx. 30 pink opaque bugle beads (2 mm)
• 1 round, gold-plated brooch mount with perforated template (1¼ in/30 mm in diameter)
• approx. 2¼ yds (2 m) nylon thread (size B)
• flat-nose pliers
• wire cutters
• scissors

1 Using the soft-flex wire and wire cutters, make several small branches, adding seed beads in whatever combination you like (use the diagrams as inspiration). You can vary the number of beads you use on each branch, and also the length of the branches, as shown in the diagrams. Always begin by using a crimp bead on the tip of each piece of wire, to keep the beads from falling off. Join several branches by threading them through a crimp bead, then crimp it with flat-nose pliers to secure the complete construction.

2 Stick each branch of beads through a hole in the brooch template. Secure them by placing a crimp bead underneath and another one on top. Hide the holes in the template by weaving through them a length of nylon thread strung with lime-green seed beads. Attach the template to the brooch back. Close the claws with flat-nose pliers.

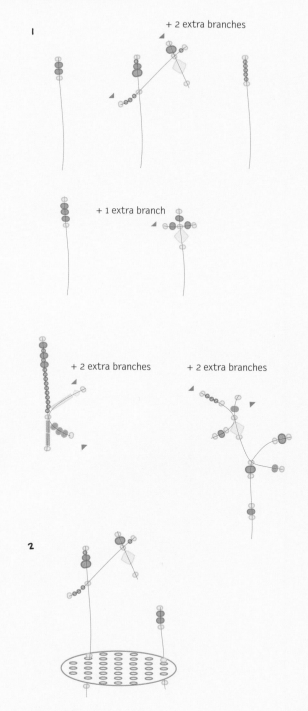

PEARLY CHAIN, instructions page 124

BUTTON BRIGHT, instructions page 125

LITTLE CHARMER, instructions page 126

FAMILY AFFAIR, instructions page 127

PEARLY CHAIN

This little chain of tiny mother-of-pearl buttons is simply joined by jump rings. The design, inspired by antique bracelets made from coins, gives it a minimalist look that echoes a baroque style.

MATERIALS
- 1 copper lobster-claw clasp
- 22 copper jump rings
- 8 square mother-of-pearl buttons (5/16 in/8 mm in diameter)
- 8 round mother-of-pearl buttons (3/8 in/10 mm in diameter)
- 1 mother-of-pearl paillette (20 mm)
- 2 flat-nose pliers

1 Attach the clasp to a jump ring, then add 1 square button to the ring. To open a jump ring, use 2 flat-nose pliers. Twist the ring gently, so as not to pull it out of shape, drawing one side of the ring towards you and the other side in the opposite direction. Proceed in the same manner to close the ring, using the 2 pliers. Continue making the bracelet, alternating 1 round button, 1 jump ring, and 1 square button, ending with a jump ring.

2 To finish, make a little chain of 5 jump rings, adding the paillette before closing the final jump ring.

VARIATION
Space out the buttons by placing more jump rings between them.

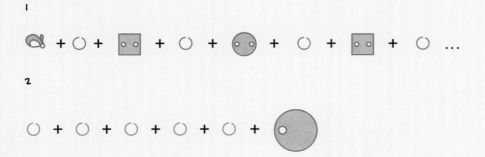

BUTTON BRIGHT

This big button bracelet will roll and jingle on your wrist. Its bright colors and rounded shapes have a touch of ethnic style and a dash of bright originality. We used vintage layered Rhodoid buttons—look for them in notion stores, thrift shops, and garage sales.

MATERIALS

- 2 silver head pins
- 1 large lobster-claw clasp
- 2 flat, silver knot covers (³/₈ in/10 mm in diameter)
- 39 in (1 m) strong, thick cotton thread
- 2 lampwork glass beads (see page 6)
- approx. 32 brightly-colored 4-hole buttons (³/₄ in/18 mm in diameter)
- 1 silver crimp bead
- 1 pink plastic hoop (1³/₈ in/35 mm in diameter)
- 2 in (5 cm) silver soft-flex wire
- 1 layered button (¹/₂ in/13 mm in diameter)
- 3 large, silver jump rings
- 2 flat-nose pliers
- round-nose pliers
- wire cutters
- scissors
- quick-drying glue

1 Take the head of a silver head pin through the hole of the knot cover. Attach the clasp by making a double loop in the stem of the pin, using round-nose pliers.

2 Cut the cotton thread in 4 equal pieces. Knot the 4 threads together at one end, then put the knot in the knot cover. Add a drop of glue and close the knot cover, using flat-nose pliers.

3 Take the 4 cotton threads through one of the lampwork beads, then string on the buttons, drawing each thread through one of the 4 holes. Thread on all the buttons, taking care not to tangle the threads and using more or less buttons to obtain the correct length for your wrist. Add the second lampwork bead.

4 Thread the crimp bead onto the piece of soft-flex wire. Pull the wire through one hole of the small button. Double over loosely, making a loop. With both ends of the wire inside the crimp bead, crimp it, and trim the wire with wire cutters. Attach the loop to one of the jump rings and add the pink plastic hoop. To open and close the ring, follow the instructions in "Pearly Chain," opposite.

5 Knot the ends of the 4 cotton threads together. Put a head pin through the hole of the second knot cover, then insert the knotted ends of the threads. Add a dab of glue and close the knot cover. Bend the end of the pin into a double loop and attach two silver jump rings. Before closing the last jump ring, slide on the jump ring with the plastic hoop and the small button.

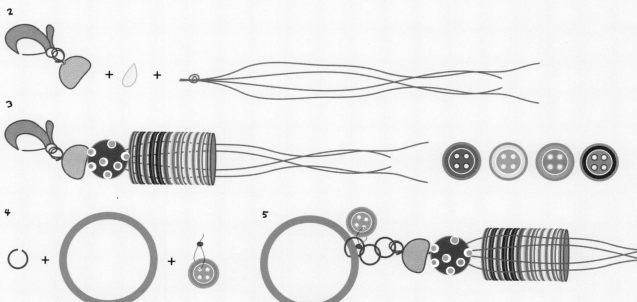

LITTLE CHARMER

A few pendants on a plain chain are all that's needed to create a simple, delicate bracelet. The copper tone of the chain, together with the light and shadow effect of the crystals, give it a slightly antique look. This is a design that can be varied in many ways.

MATERIALS

- approx. 7 in (18 cm) copper chain
- 1 copper lobster-claw clasp
- 9 copper jump rings
- 4 pink transparent faceted crystal drops (10 mm)
- 1 pale-pink opaque crystal cube (8 mm)
- 4 pale-pink opaque crystal bicones (5 mm)
- 2 pale-pink opaque crystal bicones (3 mm)
- 5 orange transparent faceted crystal beads (3 mm)
- 11 copper head pins ($5/8$ in/15 mm)
- 2 in (5 cm) fine copper chain
- 1 large-holed copper bead (5 mm)
- 1 copper eye pin
- 2 flat-nose pliers

1 Attach a jump ring to one end of the chain. Then attach the clasp. Attach 4 jump rings to the other end. To open the rings, use 2 flat-nose pliers. Twist each ring gently to open it without pulling it out of shape, pulling one side of the ring towards you and the other side in the opposite direction. Close each ring in the same way, using the 2 pliers.

2 Insert head pins through the crystal cube, the bicones, and 4 of the orange faceted beads. Using flat-nose pliers, bend the wire of each pin into a loop, without closing it completely. Slip a copper jump ring through each of the crystal drops.

3 Arrange the pendants, alternating them along the chain. Close all the loops with flat-nose pliers. Thread the copper bead onto the fine copper chain. Insert the eye pin through the remaining orange crystal and bend the wire of the pin into a loop, attaching it to the end of the fine chain before closing it completely. Attach the chain to the last jump ring.

1

2

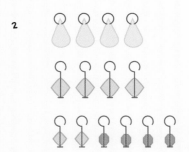

3

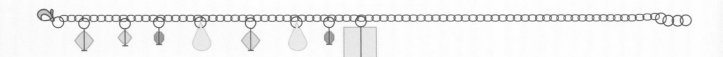

FAMILY AFFAIR

This vintage-style bracelet mounted on delicate embroidery ribbon is easily worn and will work with everything ... that's the secret of its success!

MATERIALS

- 1 silver lobster-claw clasp
- 6 silver jump rings
- 2 silver, flat ribbon crimp-ends
- 7 in (18 cm) olive-green embroidery ribbon ($\frac{1}{16}$ in/2 mm wide)
- 2 olive-green square 2-hole mother-of-pearl buttons ($\frac{1}{4}$ in/6 mm)
- 2 olive-green square 2-hole mother-of-pearl buttons ($\frac{5}{16}$ in/8 mm)
- 2 olive-green square 2-hole mother-of-pearl buttons ($\frac{3}{8}$ in/10 mm)
- 2 olive-green square 2-hole mother-of-pearl buttons ($\frac{1}{2}$ in/12 mm)
- 1 olive-green square 2-hole mother-of-pearl button ($\frac{5}{8}$ in/15 mm)
- 1 silver eye pin
- 1 freshwater pearl (5 mm)
- 2 flat-nose pliers
- scissors

I Attach the clasp to a ribbon crimp-end with a silver jump ring. To open the jump ring, use 2 flat-nose pliers, twisting the ring gently to open it without pulling it out of shape. Pull one side of the ring towards you and the other side in the opposite direction. Close the ring in the same fashion, using the 2 pliers. Slip one end of the ribbon into the crimp-end and add a dab of glue. Close the sides of the crimp-end over the ribbon.

2 Measure $1\frac{1}{4}$ in (3 cm) from the crimp-end, then make a knot. Thread the ribbon through the 2 holes of the smallest square button. Then thread it through the rest of the buttons, increasing in size to the largest, then decreasing back down in size to the smallest. When you have added the last button, make a knot. Leave $1\frac{1}{4}$ in (3 cm), trim the ribbon, then finish by fixing a crimp-end to the end of the ribbon. Make a chain of 5 jump rings. Thread the eye pin through the pearl. Trim the wire and make a loop using flat-nose pliers, taking it through the last jump ring. Close the loop.

VARIATION

This bracelet can be made using buttons that are all the same size. You could also turn it into a choker.

I

2

IMPERIAL BLUE

This glittering blue bracelet evokes the splendor of a distant, more elegant era. Its classic lines work wonders when worn casually.

MATERIALS

- 1²⁄₃ yds (1.5 m) nylon thread (size B)
- approx. 128 pale-blue seed beads (13/o)
- 11 turquoise transparent glass faceted beads (4 mm)
- 6 turquoise opaque faceted glass beads (10 mm)
- 20 blue crystal bicones (3 mm)
- scissors
- quick-drying glue

1 String 28 seed beads on the nylon thread. Double the thread and string 1 turquoise transparent faceted bead onto both threads, forming a loop of seed beads. Make sure the loop will fit around 1 of the large turquoise beads, adding or subtracting beads as necessary.

2 String 5 seed beads onto each end of the thread, then add 1 of the large turquoise opaque glass beads to only 1 thread. Cross the other thread through this bead.

3 String another 5 seed beads onto each end of the thread. Bring the two threads together and take them both through 1 turquoise transparent faceted bead.

4 String 2 blue crystals onto each thread. Bring the 2 threads together and pass them both through 1 turquoise transparent faceted bead. Repeat steps 2, 3 and 4 four times.

5 Finish by adding 5 more seed beads to each end of the thread, then cross the two ends through the last large turquoise bead. Add 1 seed bead to each end to finish the thread. Take the thread back through the large bead and knot the threads together. Add a dot of glue, allow to dry, and trim the thread.

1

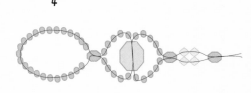

2

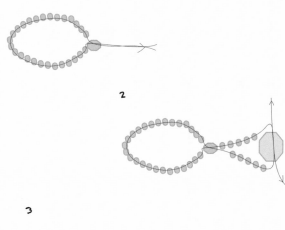

3

4

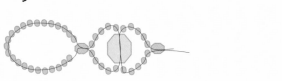

5

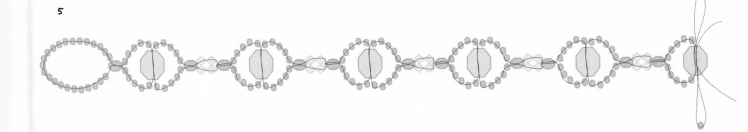

SHAKE IT UP, instructions page 134

BUTTONS GALORE, instructions page 135

CANDY STORE, instructions page 136

DAZZLING STITCHES, instructions page 137

SHAKE IT UP

Soft colors and pearly reflections combine with charms that jingle discreetly, making a pretty accompaniment to the slightest movement of your wrist.

MATERIALS

- 6¼–7 in (16–18 cm) gray-blue embroidery ribbon (³/₁₆ in/4 mm)
- 2 silver clamshell knot covers
- 1 silver spring clasp
- 3 silver head pins
- 1 silver eye pin
- 3 lime-green sequins (¼ in/6 mm)
- 1 pale-green, round 2-hole mother-of-pearl button (1 in/25 mm in diameter)
- 1 lime-green, oval 2-hole mother-of-pearl button (½ in/12 mm in diameter)
- 1 dark-green, oval 2-hole mother of pearl button (½ in/12 mm in diameter)
- 1 sky-blue, oval 2-hole mother-of-pearl button (⅝ in/15 mm in diameter)
- 3 large, silver crimp beads

- flat-nose pliers
- round-nose pliers
- wire cutters
- scissors
- quick-drying glue

1 Make a knot at one end of the ribbon and place it in a knot cover. Add a drop of glue and close the knot cover. Attach the knot cover to one side of the clasp. Leave 2¾ in (7 cm) of ribbon, then make a double knot.

2 Thread 1 sequin, 1 oval button, and 1 large crimp bead onto a head pin. Using round-nose pliers, loop the head pin through the second hole of the button then through the crimp bead. Crimp it with flat-nose pliers. Repeat this step with the other 2 oval buttons.

3 Pass the eye pin through a hole in the large round button from underneath. Hang from it the 3 little charms you have made with the oval buttons. Using round-nose pliers, bend the wire of the eye pin and pass it through the second buttonhole. Using wire cutters, trim the wire to ³/₈ in (10 mm) above the button and make a little loop to match the eye.

4 Thread the ribbon through the two loops you have made at the back of the large button. Secure the button with a double knot. Leave 2¾ in (7 cm) of plain ribbon and knot the end, trim and attach a knot cover. Add a dab of glue and close the knot cover. Add the other half of the clasp to finish.

1

2

3

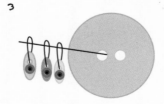
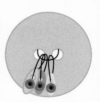

4

BUTTONS GALORE

This staggered arrangement of adorable, little round buttons is almost sculptural in appearance. Their size, iridescence, and color make them look like delicate beads.

MATERIALS
- 17 in (44 cm) suede-leather cord (¹⁄₁₆ in/2 mm wide)
- 33 small plastic buttons with back hooks, in assorted colors
- scissors

I Measure 5 in (13 cm) from one end of the cord, then make a double knot. String on the buttons, arranging them in a staggered pattern from front to back. Secure them with a double knot at the end of the bracelet. Leave 5 in (13 cm) of cord, then trim off.

VARIATIONS
Go thrifting: You'll find lots of vintage buttons with hooks. This very simple bracelet can also be adapted as a choker.

I

CANDY STORE

This sassy, sinuous bracelet sports delicious acid-drop colors. The hollow plastic lacing plays matchmaker, uniting many strands that look like rows of candy.

I

2

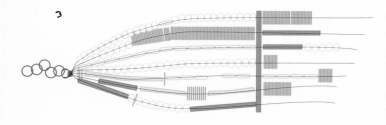

3

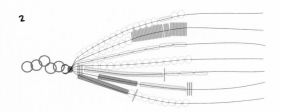

4

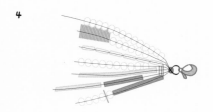

MATERIALS

- 1 silver lobster-claw clasp
- 7 lengths of nylon thread (size B), each $6^{1}/_{4}$–7 in (16–18 cm) long
- 2 silver crimp beads
- approx. 500 small, fluorescent-pink transparent sequins ($^{1}/_{8}$ in/3 mm in diameter)
- approx. 6 in (15 cm) lime-green plastic lacing (see page 9)
- approx. $7^{1}/_{4}$ in (18 cm) red plastic lacing
- approx. 180 white pearl seed beads (13/0)
- approx. 40 white opaque seed beads (8/0)
- approx. 50 white pearl bugle beads
- sewing needle
- flat-nose pliers
- scissors

I Pass the 7 lengths of thread through a crimp bead and the loop of the clasp. Pass the ends back through the crimp bead and crimp it with flat-nose pliers.

2 Add different items (sequins, bugle beads, seed beads, lengths of plastic lacing) to each thread for $2^{1}/_{4}$ in (6 cm).

3 Using a sewing needle, pierce a $1^{1}/_{2}$ in- (4 cm-) length of plastic lacing seven times at regular intervals, and draw each of the 7 threads through one of the holes. Continue alternating different items (sequins, bugle beads, seed beads, lengths of plastic lacing) for another $2^{1}/_{4}$ in (6 cm). Draw the 7 threads through another $1^{1}/_{2}$ in- (4 cm-) piece of pierced, red plastic lacing. Finish by alternating the beads and other items for another $2^{1}/_{4}$ in (6 cm).

4 Close the bracelet by adding 1 crimp bead to the 7 threads. Pass the threads through the loop of the other end of the clasp and back through the crimp bead. Crimp with flat-nose pliers, and trim off the thread.

DAZZLING STITCHES

A few sequins and beads embroidered onto a simple ribbon create a poetic theme to wear on your wrist. You could also use this method to make a floral motif.

MATERIALS

- 1 gold-tone lobster-claw clasp
- 2 gold-tone jump rings
- 2 flat, gold-tone ribbon crimp-ends (1¼ in/30 mm)
- 6¾–7½ in (17–19 cm) sheer ribbon (1¼ in/30 mm wide)
- 15 seed beads, in different colors and finishes
- 3 red sequins (⅜ in/10 mm in diameter)
- 5 green opaque sequins (6 mm in diameter)
- 5 orange opaque sequins (6 mm in diameter)
- red Polyester sewing thread
- embroidery needle
- 2 flat-nose pliers
- scissors
- quick-drying glue

I Attach the clasp to a jump ring. To open the jump ring, use 2 flat-nose pliers and twist the ring gently to open it without pulling it out of shape. Pull one side of the ring towards you and the other side in the opposite direction. Close the ring in the same way, using the 2 pliers. Next, attach the ribbon crimp-ends by turning back a small hem at one end of the ribbon and placing it in the crimp-end. Add a drop of glue and close. Repeat at the other end of the ribbon, cutting it first to the correct size to fit your wrist.

2 Using an embroidery needle and red Polyester thread, compose your design by sewing the beads and sequins on the ribbon.

I

2

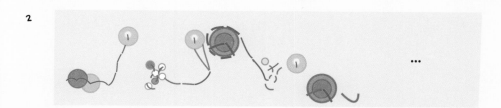

NIGHT MUSIC

The elegance of this design owes as much to the delicacy of the mesh as to the glitter of the deep black beads. Stitch it around evening gloves or extend the design and wear it as a choker.

MATERIALS

Motif 1
• 2 yds (1.8 m) black jewelry wire (size 0)
• approx. 74 black faceted Czech glass beads (3 mm)
• approx. 112 black matte opaque seed beads (11/0)
• wire cutters

Fastening loop
• 16 in (40 cm) black jewelry wire (size 0)
• approx. 35 black matte opaque seed beads

Fastening bobble
• 28 in (70 cm) black jewelry wire (size 0)
• approx. 28 black faceted Czech glass beads (3 mm)
• approx. 40 black matte opaque seed beads (11/0)
• wire cutters

Motif 2
• 1³/₄ yds (1.6 m) black jewelry wire (size 0)
• approx. 20 black faceted Czech glass beads (3 mm)
• approx. 270 black matte opaque seed beads
• wire cutters

To make Motif 1

1 Thread 4 seed beads and 4 faceted glass beads onto the jewelry wire alternately, starting with a seed bead. Slide them to the center of the wire, then fold it, crossing one end of the wire through the last 3 beads. You should now have 2 rows.

2 Thread 1 seed bead onto one end of the wire, and 1 seed bead, 1 faceted glass bead, 1 seed bead, and 1 faceted glass bead onto the other end. Pass the first wire through the last 3 beads. Continue like this until you have made 37 rows (approximately 6½ in/17 cm of the motif). Finish by taking the wires back through the beads several times. Trim off with wire cutters.

To make the fastening loop

3 Pass the 16 in- (40 cm-) length of wire through the 3 beads of the first row of Motif 1. Thread 3 seed beads on each end of the wire. Add another seed bead to one end and cross the wires through this bead. Add 2 seed beads to each wire. Cross the wires through a last bead, making a loop. Thread 24 seed beads on one end of the wire and secure the wires by taking them back through the loop.

To make the fastening bobble

4 Using 16 in (40 cm) of the wire and following the instructions for Motif 1, make 10 rows. When you have made the last row, take the wires back through the 3 beads in the first row to make a bobble. Take them back again through different beads. Trim off the wires.

MOTIF 1

1   **2**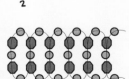

FASTENING LOOP

3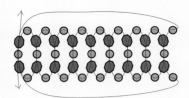

FASTENING BOBBLE

4

CONTINUED >

5

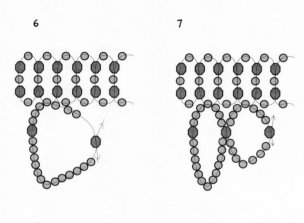

MOTIF 2

6   **7**

8

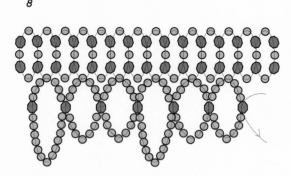

5 To attach the bobble, draw the remaining 12 in (30 cm) of wire through the 3 beads of the last row of Motif 1 and center it. Add 3 seed beads to each end of the wire. Add another seed bead to one end and cross the wires through it. Add another 2 seed beads to each end of the wire. Add a last seed bead to one end and cross the wires through it to make a loop. Take both the wires through a bead in the bobble and secure by drawing each wire through several other beads, then trim off.

To make Motif 2

6 Pass the remaining black jewelry wire through the second seed bead in the bottom row of Motif 1, leaving an equal length on each side of the bead. Add 3 seed beads to one wire. String 3 seed beads, 1 faceted bead, 13 seed beads, and 1 faceted bead onto the other wire. Cross the first wire through this last bead, to make a large loop.

7 String 3 seed beads onto the wire next to the necklace, take the wire through a seed bead in Motif 1, then add 3 seed beads and 1 faceted bead. Add 7 seed beads to the other wire. Cross the wires through the faceted bead to make a small loop.

8 Repeat steps 6 and 7, alternating 1 large loop with 2 small ones, systematically passing one end of the wire through a bead in Motif 1. Finish by taking each wire back through the beads several times, and trim off.

HINT

To speed up your work, use a store-bought clasp, instead of making the loop and bobble.

LIST OF PROJECTS

ACKNOWLEDGMENTS

A box of precious jewels to Sophie for her enthusiasm.

A million "seed beads" to the entire Marabout team for giving me carte blanche.

Bags of crystal beads to Virginie, for her great editorial partnership.

Rhinestones and sequins to Akiko, Christian, and Pierre.

Lots of cabochons to Cécile.

A shower of buttons to Frédéric for his energy, and to Rose for her starry eyes.

And bead necklaces to all, near or far, who have contributed to the making of this book.

PROPS AND ACCESSORIES

H&M: sweaters pp. 25, 42, 73, 74, 101, 132; t-shirts pp. 62, 114, 130; shirt p. 99.

MUJI: boxes pp. 32, 33, 48, 75, 90, 94, 103, 118, 125; display shelf p. 39; jeans pp. 42, 52, 60, 130, 132; bag p. 114.

CAMAÏEU: shirts pp. 60, 93; sweaters pp. 80, 115; dress p. 104.

All of the photographs in this book were taken by Akiko Ida,
except those on p. 3, 43, 55, 66, 82, 83, 89, 94, 111, 128, 131, 142, 143, 144,
which were taken by Pierre Javelle

Shopping and photo styling: Christian Kleeman

Editorial coordinator: Virginie Mahieux-Mahoudeau

Published in the United States by Potter Craft, an imprint of the
Crown Publishing Group, a division of Random House, Inc., New York.
www.crownpublishing.com
www.clarksonpotter.com

Originally published in France as *Des Perles et des Bijoux* by
Marabout (Hachette Livre), Paris, in 2005.
Copyright © 2005 by Marabout

POTTER CRAFT and CLARKSON N. POTTER are trademarks, and POTTER and colophon
are registered trademarks of Random House, Inc.

Library of Congress Cataloging-in-Publication Data is available

ISBN-10 0-307-34572-6
ISBN-13 978-0-307-34572-1

Printed in Singapore

10 9 8 7 6 5 4 3 2 1

First American Edition